# Decent Aid

# Decent Aid

*An Introduction to Ethics
in Philanthropy*

DAVID MUTEMWA

*foreword by Michal Opatrný*

☙PICKWICK *Publications* · Eugene, Oregon

DECENT AID
An Introduction to Ethics in Philanthropy

Copyright © 2025 David Mutemwa. All rights reserved. Except for brief quotations in critical publications or reviews, no part of this book may be reproduced in any manner without prior written permission from the publisher. Write: Permissions, Wipf and Stock Publishers, 199 W. 8th Ave., Suite 3, Eugene, OR 97401.

Pickwick Publications
An Imprint of Wipf and Stock Publishers
199 W. 8th Ave., Suite 3
Eugene, OR 97401

www.wipfandstock.com

PAPERBACK ISBN: 979-8-3852-2507-1
HARDCOVER ISBN: 979-8-3852-2508-8
EBOOK ISBN: 979-8-3852-2509-5

*Cataloguing-in-Publication data:*

Names: Mutemwa, David, author. | Opatrný, Michal, 1978–, foreword.

Title: Decent aid : an introduction to ethics in philanthropy / David Mutemwa ; foreword by Michal Opatrný.

Description: Eugene, OR : Pickwick Publications, 2025 | Includes bibliographical references and index.

Identifiers: ISBN 979-8-3852-2507-1 (paperback) | ISBN 979-8-3852-2508-8 (hardcover) | ISBN 979-8-3852-2509-5 (ebook)

Subjects: LCSH: Charities—Moral and ethical aspects.

Classification: HV41 .M87 2025 (paperback) | HV41 .M87 (ebook)

07/22/25

*Dedication*

This book is dedicated to all philanthropists, humanitarians, charitable organizations, scholars, practitioners, and policymakers who are interested in philanthropic activities in developing regions of the world, especially in Africa. Above all, I dedicate this book to the wellbeing of the individual and society as well as better cognition of the world, humans, and God.

# Contents

*Foreword by Michal Opatrný* | *ix*

*Acknowledgments* | *xii*

*Abbreviations* | *xiii*

*Introduction* | *xv*

1     The Issue | 1
2     Operationalization of Charitable Organizations | 9
3     Literature Survey | 21
4     The Approach | 53
5     Showing the Workings | 65
6     Model for Ethical Evaluation of Philanthropic Strategies | 102
7     Concluding Perspectives | 137

*Bibliography* | *143*

*Index* | *155*

# Foreword

DECENT AID IS EXPECTED when speaking generally about aid, helping professions or organizations. We expect the same from various actors and sectors such as the pastoral ministry, social work provision, education, and healthcare. To be decent while working with people goes without saying. We are, therefore, even more surprised by the unethical transactions that take place during aid provision. This is not only a matter of abuse of interpersonal relationships, i.e., abusing the client's need or, on the other hand, abusing the help, but also a matter of charitable organizations acting more or less ethically in their projects. Like the individual, the organization can also follow its particular goals, which may not always be consistent with the welfare of its clients. This book—*Decent Aid: An Introduction to Ethics in Philanthropy*—by David Mutemwa focuses significantly on a very topical field of aid provision in Africa and attempts to contribute towards making aid provision an ethical matter.

David was my PhD student at the University of South Bohemia, České Budějovice, and this book is based on his dissertation titled "An Ethical Evaluation of Philanthropic Strategies Employed by Charitable Organizations Operating in the Mongu District of Western Zambia." David's dissertation was based on our PhD program, formerly called Charity Studies but later changed to Spirituality and Ethics in Social Work. This program is oriented around the interdisciplinary and transdisciplinary research topics that border on Social Work and Humanities, particularly Theology and Ethics. Thus, the issue of decent aid in the Zambian context fits very well in this program. The idea behind researching this topic was inspired by David's personal and professional experience in Mongu district of Western Zambia. This led him to delve deeper into the issue and come out with a wider perspective beyond just his experience.

# Foreword

Therefore, the book you are about to read is about ethics in philanthropy. It is based on desk reviews and field research. What gives the book exceptional rigor is that it is not common in the field of Ethics to combine the approaches of Art and Humanities on one hand, with Social Science research on the other. If these two are combined, the judgment on the social research findings would be made from the normative point of view of ethics. Not so in this book by David Mutemwa. He is providing research from historical, legal, ethical, philosophical, and theological perspectives, as well as perspectives from the field of social sciences, to delineate his topic.

He has also conducted in-depth empirical social research (interviews with CEOs of international and local charitable organizations who were available, as well as local formal and informal authorities) about philanthropic activities in the Mongu district. It is worthy appreciating David's intention to focus on philanthropic activities from the point of view of their reception by local communities. He was very interested in their ethical perspectives of philanthropic activities and strategies of both home and international aid organizations. David succeeded in this and, therefore, you can also read in this book his very embodied ethical evaluation of philanthropic strategies of different charitable organizations operating in Mongu. Consequently, based on his research findings, he has also made theoretical conclusions and very practical suggestions for future praxis, which are set in the field of the current discourse of social sciences. This makes his findings accessible, especially for helping professions like social, development, and humanitarian workers, as well as the management of philanthropic organizations.

Besides this book by David Mutemwa being significant in the respective current field of discourse and research, it also highlights one more particular issue; his research work interconnects the global and local perspectives as he has not only evaluated the situation in a specific African context from a Western perspective, but also from a regional standpoint. He has exposed the global influence on the African region of Mongu exerted through international charitable organizations operating in Zambia. He, however, employs a combination of Western theories and methodological approaches with traditional African philosophy (Ubuntu) to achieve this goal. This makes it possible to understand the ethical dimensions of philanthropic strategies in an African context from a Western perspective, thereby helping charitable organizations to avoid implementing strategies that could be unethical from the local perspective. This is very important for European and American charitable organizations as it guides them in the best practices to adopt while implementing their projects in an African context such as Zambia.

This approach in David's research was greatly facilitated by the fact that neither Czechia nor the former Austro-Hungarian Empire, of which Czechia was a part, was ever a colonial superpower. Rather, by working together with David, we were able to share different cultural experiences of foreign interference. Thus, in addition to the British colonization of Zambia, whose heritage is the cultural experience of David, my experience of the Russian-Soviet colonization of Eastern Europe and the Czech Republic facilitated a significant part of the work.

Therefore, from the point of view of importance for contemporary research, *Decent Aid* significantly contributes to the decolonization and strengthening of relations between Europe, America and Africa. Moreover, this book is also important for local stakeholders and authorities in Mongu specifically and Zambia in general. Additionally, it is important for other African countries to know how to observe, research, and evaluate the impact of the West, made by the international charitable organizations operating within their communities. This approach is also valuable for the evaluation of philanthropic strategies of local charitable organizations.

I am really pleased that Wipf and Stock Publishers were interested in this book. In this way, the book interconnects three continents and, as I am convinced, benefits of all the people on the respective continents. I believe academia's primary task is to share knowledge and competencies and mutually exchange different ideas and approaches to better comprehension of the world and humans, as well as the universe and God. David Mutemwa's *Decent Aid* is the next important part of this mosaic of knowledge, and I hope readers will look and walk with this book beyond the horizon of their existing ideas.

Michal Opatrný
Associate Professor for Pastoral Theology, Caritas Studies, & Social Work.
Dean: Faculty of Theology—University of South Bohemia in České Budějovice, Czech Republic.

# Acknowledgments

I HEREBY ACKNOWLEDGE the immense contribution of Associate Professor Dr. Michal Opatrný who was the supervisor for my dissertation work that forms the basis for this book, and he also wrote the foreword. I equally acknowledge Associate Professor Dr. Rudolf Svoboda and Associate Professor Dr. Robert Doyle for endorsing this book. Rudolf was Chairperson of the committee for my doctoral defense while Robert was one of the opponents for my defense. I thank them all for their positive criticism that helped me to fine-tune the contents that have now been published in this book.

Finally and equally important, I sincerely acknowledge the University of South Bohemia in České Budějovice, Czech Republic, for the financial support they rendered through the Faculty of Theology to cover the publication costs for this book.

# Abbreviations

NGO        Non Governmental Organization
FBO        Faith-Based Organization

# Introduction

THE PRESENCE OF CHARITABLE organizations in developing countries such as Zambia dates as way back as the nineteenth century, but still very little has been known about their ethical obligations and operating strategies among the communities in which they operate, mainly due to lack of relevant national governing policies of the respective host countries.[1] Accordingly, this book is written from the author's lived experience and original doctoral study, prompted by the fact that next to nothing was known about the ethical aspects and operating strategies of charitable organizations in his home town of Mongu and country of Zambia at large, despite an influx of such organizations among the local communities since the precolonial era. Even as an independent country, "Zambia has had no national policy to govern the NGO sector," which includes charities, despite the ever increasing numbers of NGOs (Non-Governmental Organizations) in the country since the 1850s.[2] It is, therefore, not known to what extent the ethical obligations of charitable organizations in the country are honored or dishonored in the implementation of their philanthropic strategies.

According to the just cited Zambian government source in the respective footnote, a Non-Governmental Organization is a

> private voluntary grouping of individuals or associations, whether corporate or unincorporated, not established or operated for profit, partisan politics or any commercial purposes and whom or which have organised themselves for the promotion of civic education, advocacy, human rights, social welfare, development, charity, research or other activity or program meant for the benefit

---

1. Banks and Hulme, *Role of NGOs and Civil Society*, 3; Hasnan et al., *Issues, Challenges, and the Way Forward*, 777; Mweene, "Assessment of Community Participation," 7.

2. MCDSS, *National Policy on Non-Governmental Organisations*, 1–2.

# Introduction

or interest of the public through resources mobilized from sources within or outside Zambia.

In accordance with this definition, the terms charitable organization and NGO are appropriately and interchangeably used in this book as charitable organizations are commonly known as NGOs in Zambia and probably other African countries too. The last cited government source is the first and only exclusive policy document so far on the governance of NGOs in Zambia published in April 2018, although it was still undergoing scrutiny and did not contain an explicit ethical code of conduct for NGOs operating in the country. There is, therefore, a definite gap for which this book is set to make a valuable contribution.

The town of Mongu was identified as the local context for the case study because of its paradoxical combination of characteristics, vis-à-vis relatively smaller population than most other parts of the country, vast land surface area, chronic high poverty levels, and an influx of charitable NGOs. Although the research findings are valid within their specific time, space, and value context,[3] Nancy Burns and Susan Grove[4] also observe that by understanding the meaning of a phenomenon in its context, it becomes rather easier to understand phenomena in other similar contexts. As such, an ethical evaluation of philanthropic strategies employed by charitable organizations in Mongu district will also help to enlighten the wider context of the country on the ethical issues at stake elsewhere charitable organizations are operating, especially that the problematic praxis under study applies to the broader context as well, both nationally and globally as will be seen in the following chapters.

---

3. Botes, "Functional Approach in Nursing Research," 22.
4. Burns and Grove, *Practice of Nursing Research*, 29.

# 1

# The Issue

EVERY ISSUE HAS A BACKGROUND and context. So, to understand the issue at hand more comprehensively and accurately, it is better to precede with a brief presentation of the background contexts that triggered the case study that subsequently formed the basis of this book.

## BACKGROUND

The case study was conducted in the interior of Africa in an inland town of Mongu, which is the capital of the Western Province of Zambia, an inland country too. As at the time of the study, the town of Mongu had an estimated human population of 179,585, according to the official publication of the then last National Census of Housing and Population conducted in 2010.[1] With a land surface area of about 6,360 square kilometers, the population density of Mongu was estimated at 28 people per square kilometer. According to the 2015 Living Conditions Monitoring Survey Report by the Central Statistical Office,[2] about 80 percent of the people in Mongu and all Western Province were living in abject poverty due to a combination of

---

1. CSO, *2010 Census*, 47. Cf. Currently, the population of Mongu is estimated to be 197,816 according to the latest census of population and housing conducted in 2022, after the study was already concluded, which is still a small population (https://www.zamstats.gov.zm/wp-content/uploads/2023/12/2022-Census-of-Population-and-Housing-Preliminary.pdf).

2. CSO, *2015 Living Conditions*, 11, 115.

factors, including lack of capacity to procure agricultural inputs, very low wages, and lack of capital and credit facilities to start their own businesses.

Stunningly, there were about fifty registered NGOs operating in the town as at the time when the study was conducted.[3] Although most of those NGOs were involved with sensitive groups such as orphaned and vulnerable children, women, and the physically challenged or differently abled, very little, if not nothing, was known about their ethical obligations and operational strategies in the communities, shockingly not even by the oversight government institutions.[4] As per the last cited source, Zambia's Ministry of Community Development and Social Services had just been tasked to spearhead the formulation and implementation of the National NGO Policy as at the time of the research for this book. Among others, the ministry was going to register all local and international NGOs operating in Zambia and facilitate the constitution and operations of the envisaged NGO Registration Board.

Such a paradoxical situation as just described is what prompted me to register and institute a systematic inquiry into the ethical aspects of philanthropic strategies employed by charitable organizations such as were operating in Mongu district of Western Zambia. The findings and model developed from the study are useful also to the country of Zambia and African continent because the issue being addressed involves local and wider contextual factors. In fact, it cannot be effectively addressed at local level without taking into consideration the national and international factors that have practically influenced the local situation.

It is commonplace to argue that even though a country has no policy to govern NGOs, such as was the case with Zambia from the pre-colonial era, it is still imperative to evaluate the ethical aspects of philanthropic strategies employed by charitable organizations through ethical reflection on universal ethical principles in order to allow the respective organizations and moral communities to test their practices and norms against universally acceptable ethical standards. "Ethical reflection" is the use of ethical principles, rules, or guidelines to guide action toward moral ends.[5] This comes close to developing normative perspectives on boundary issues that cannot be crossed by our discourse of various episodes, situations, and contexts. Mel Thompson writes that "when thinking about any problem it

3. MCDSS, *NGO File 2018*.
4. MCDSS, *National Policy*, 1, 7–9.
5. Osmer, *Practical Theology*, 161.

is important to start by establishing own foundational values, which are principles that you are unwilling to compromise."⁶ This is not a matter of importing ethics into the problematic praxis or research, but rather the recognition that ethical norms and values already are part of any project process.⁷ And the application of such ethical norms and values does not only occur at the end of a project, but is present from the outset and influences it throughout.⁸

Suffice it to extrapolate that the town of Mongu and nation of Zambia situation is not happening in a vacuum, but involves both local and global concepts, a situation that Ed Stetzar and David Putman rightly coined as the emerging "glocal concept" to signify the interplay of global and local concepts in a given situation.⁹ Insights from social sciences portray the world as an individual whole and web of relationships in which every action has complex, non-linear and unpredictable effects.¹⁰ Hence the theme of the case study had to deal with the uniqueness of the ethical aspects of philanthropic strategies employed by charitable organizations operating in Mongu district and Zambia, while being aware of the presence of global traits within the local situation. As already mentioned, understanding the meaning of a phenomenon in its context makes it easier to understand phenomena in other similar contexts as similar trends and patterns are perceived to be replayed in different contexts and at different levels of societal life. Roy Bhaskar provides a befitting analysis that the world is in a complex of crises involving ecological problems, social interactions among people, unequal distribution of wealth and resources, and social justice.¹¹ This is true for the world of NGOs too.

For instance, a research by Simon Kang'ethe, professor of social work and social development at the University of Fort Hare, and Tatenda Manomano reveals that charitable NGOs in Africa were weakened by funding challenges, corruption and embezzlement of funds, especially by the top brass management, poor synergy and poor collaboration between the NGOs and the government, as well as inadequacy of skilled labor force.¹² In

---

6. Thompson, *Understanding Ethics* [5th ed.], 107.
7. Osmer, *Practical Theology*, 149.
8. Browning, *Fundamental Practical Theology*, 39.
9. Stetzar and Putman, *Breaking the Missional Code*, 5.
10. Korac-Kakabadse et al., "Spirituality and Leadership Praxis," 166.
11. Placenza, "Interview with Roy Bhaskar."
12. Kang'ethe and Manomano, "Exploring the Challenges," 1495.

Zimbabwe, Elvin Shava's research revealed that NGOs struggled to uphold accountability in their poverty alleviation strategies due to poor governance structures, limited skills, political interference, and poor monitoring and evaluation techniques.[13] Owolabi Akintola's research into NGO accountability and sustainable development in Nigeria reveals a hierarchical conception of accountability that privileges a narrow range of stakeholders, which is short-term in focus and not strategic as the target communities remain unaware of details that they should have to both benefit from and collaborate appropriately with NGOs that operate in their communities.[14] Even in countries outside Africa such as in Malaysia research has shown that the information contained in the reports by charities was insufficient and misrepresentative for effective monitoring and regulation of the respective charitable organizations.[15] It is, therefore, commonplace to rationalize that there are global trends being replayed in a given local situation pertaining to the ethicality of philanthropic strategies of charitable organizations operating among poor African communities. While there is strong theoretical backing for promoting accountability among NGOs, especially within the African context, Ronelle Burger and Dineo Seabe comment that there is little evidence to suggest that the dominant models of accountability have been successful in promoting ethical behaviour, transparency, and effectiveness among NGOs operating in Africa.[16]

It is against the foregoing backdrop that I was prompted to undertake a systematic evaluation of the subject hereby under discourse in order to come up with a practical model for evaluating the ethicality of such NGOs as operate among poor African communities.

## CORE ISSUE

In view of the foregoing background information, the core of the issue at hand is that next to nothing was known about the ethical aspects and operating strategies of charitable organizations operating among most poor African communities despite an influx of such organizations in the respective areas for prolonged years as the case with Mongu town in Western Zambia. In addition, even at national level, some countries like Zambia have had

---

13. Shava, "Accountability of Non-Governmental Organisations," 122.
14. Akintola, "NGO Accountability," 67.
15. Hasnan et al., *Issues, Challenges*, 777.
16. Burger and Seabe, "NGO Accountability in Africa," 77.

no policy to govern charitable organizations, despite the presence of such organizations in the country since the nineteenth century.[17] As such, I was inevitably prompted to probe the ethical aspects of charitable organizations such as were operating in Mongu district and the extent to which such aspects were honored or dishonored in the implementation of the charities' philanthropic strategies.

Charitable organizations are no different in the need to foster ethics, given their public service mission.[18] According to the just cited co-authors in the footnote, ethics may comparatively be more important to charities than non-charitable organizations. Hence one can argue that charitable organizations have an even bigger stake in creating and maintaining a positive public image than private enterprises because their primary stakeholders are donors. The "donors" are individual persons or organizations who donate money, services, and goods to assist an organization with its mission and provide operating funds.[19] Donors do this without the incentives of dividends, ownership or other such returns as those afforded by shareholders of public listed companies.

It is, nevertheless, important for donors to donate responsibly and reasonably. Said another way, donors should donate ethically. In his article titled, "An ethical guide to responsible giving," Ted Lechterman highlights six key ethical guidelines to what he calls responsible giving, namely: giving from the heart, giving to the neediest, giving mindfully, giving to heal and address injustices, giving to overcome unjust policies, and mixing and matching.[20] The last guiding point (mixing and matching) is a reflection on the preceding five guidelines and an observation that there is no single school of thought that offers a perfect guide to responsible giving. According to Hennie Swanepoel and Frik de Beer's work on community development and breaking the cycle of poverty,[21] it is also ethically required of charities to coordinate their philanthropic efforts in order to optimize their impact and avoid duplicity. Despite the divergent opinions, Ted Lechterman points out that scholars who espouse these different schools of thought still agree on one thing, namely that donors should reflect more on their giving

---

17. MCDSS, *National Policy*, 1–2.
18. Hasnan et al., *Issues, Challenges*, 777.
19. Cambridge English Dictionary, "Donor"; Hasnan et al., *Issues, Challenges*, 777.
20. Lechterman, "Ethical Guide to Responsible Giving."
21. Swanepoel and Beer, *Community Development*, 41.

decisions. By extension, thinking more about what it means to be a charity will help a donor to give more ethically.

On the other end it has also been proven that most recipients of charitable aid, especially in remote areas of Africa, do not have the necessary skills, knowledge, and training to work with charitable organizations.[22] As such they are naïve, vulnerable, and prone to socio-cultural deceptions and intellectual abuse in cases of unethical philanthropic strategies implemented by unchecked charitable organizations in their communities. Laurence Kirmayer and others once wrote that "Around the world, indigenous people have experienced rapid culture changes, marginalization, and absorption into a global economy with little regard for their autonomy."[23] This sort of vulnerability can cause indignant communities to be sceptical about participating in modern transformational development projects that are implemented by charitable organizations. Therefore, it is imperative to consider the ethical implications at stake in the application of philanthropic strategies by charitable organizations operating among rural African communities.

An overarching question in the ethical evaluation of charities is whether a charity works and achieves results in an ethically acceptable manner. In analyzing what makes a good charity, Ruth Gripper and Lona Joy[24] write that evidence of results only indicates to what extent a charity is making a difference and how this improves over time, as well as inform judgment of the value for money. The ethical aspect is, however, not satisfied with evidence of results only because it is not true that the end always justifies the means.[25] For instance, it has been argued that the information reported by charities could be insufficient or misrepresentative for effective monitoring and regulation of the respective charities.[26] Ethical satisfaction requires that both the means and the end be acceptable.[27] Said another way, if the premise be acceptable, then the conclusion is also acceptable.

I hereby accept, for the purpose of this publication, that charitable organizations have a critical role to play in the development of society,

---

22. Mutemwa, "Effectiveness of Sesheke Church," 169.
23. Kirmayer et al., *Mental Health of Indigenous Peoples*, 5.
24. Gripper and Joy, *What Makes a Good Charity?*, 23.
25. Magnus, *Age of Aging*, 136; Natter, "Do the Ends Justify the Means"; Touré-Tillery and Fishbach, "End Justifies the Means," 1.
26. Hasnan et al., *Issues, Challenges*, 777.
27. Nordquist, "Premises and Conclusions."

## The Issue

improvement of communities, and promotion of citizen participation.[28] The focus of this book, however, is to evaluate the praxis and impact of ethical aspects of philanthropic strategies employed by charitable organizations in improving the lives of the local people and community as a whole. By default, I will also endeavor to decipher how the challenges and lessons learnt from this particular case study are significantly connected to, or isolated from, similar situations globally, especially in Africa.

Philanthropic strategies in this case entail alleviating the plight of the poor and less privileged local people in an ethically acceptable manner.[29] This is in accordance with the primary concept of philanthropy that is also upheld by religious teachings of human wellbeing, the good life, good society, and transformation of the world.[30] For instance, the Christian biblical teaching in Matthew 25:35–40 urges humans to attend to the needs of the vulnerable and less privileged people in society. Commenting on the just mentioned Christian pericope, Tokunboh Adeyemo, chief editor of the first Bible commentary based on Africa, ultimately states that Christians are supposed to respond to human needs in a holistic manner.[31] Likewise, Thomas Hale also in his work on *The Applied New Testament Commentary* writes concerning the same portion of Scripture that Christians should serve Christ by attending to the needs of others, especially those who are poor and less privileged.[32]

"Ethicality" in this case is perceived to be the desired means of effecting philanthropic strategies of charitable organizations operating among poor African communities such as Mongu district in Western Zambia. It entails decency in the way philanthropic aid is channeled to the intended end users. In view of the foregoing explication of the background and core issue at hand, the concept of ethics in philanthropy in essence entails a total evaluation of charitable organizations' strategies toward alleviating the plight of the poor populace. Therefore, it requires a holistic approach to all other relevant contextual issues such as poverty alleviation, lifestyle, religious ethics, social justice, and politics.

So far, the background and problematic praxis with ethics in philanthropy have been discussed in order to present the contexts that called for

28. Candid, "What Is an NGO?"
29. Magnus, *Age of Aging*, 136.
30. Wet, *Understanding Transformational Development*, 7–8.
31. Adeyemo, *Africa Bible Commentary*, 1164.
32. Hale, *Applied New Testament Commentary*, 121.

the issue of this book. In order to conduct an appropriate and effective ethical evaluation of philanthropic strategies of charitable organizations, it is imperative also to operationalize charitable organizations and identify the types of such organizations that operate among African communities.

# 2

# Operationalization of Charitable Organizations

## INTRODUCTION

This chapter operationalizes the charitable organizations operating in rural African communities and related concepts in order to come up with an appropriate ethical evaluation of philanthropic strategies employed by the said charities. In social sciences, the term *operationalization* means the process through which abstract concepts are translated into measurable variables.[1] Accordingly, the process involves breaking down the abstract concepts into manageable components, making rational decisions, and legitimating such decisions as in respect of theoretical considerations. The concepts to be dealt with in this chapter include charity, charitable organizations and such types as are operating in rural African communities, charity law, and theoretical framework for the ethical evaluation of philanthropic strategies employed by charitable organizations.

## ETYMOLOGY OF CHARITY

In order to establish a proper basis for the ethical evaluation of philanthropic strategies employed by charitable organizations, it is necessary also to investigate the origin of the concept of charity and how its meaning has

---

1. Harvey, "Social Research Glossary."

possibly evolved over time. Alexis Garcia-Irons[2] writes that somewhere in the mid-1800s, establishments called charitable organizations were set up in England and they comprised church personnel and volunteers who were designated to render help to the poor, homeless, and severely ill people in society. According to the just cited author, the principles underlying these early social work practices were founded on the biblical idea of charity.

The word *charity* has its roots in the Bible and it underpins the praxis of *Diakonia* in Protestant theology, while in Catholic theology it embraces the concept of *Caritas Theory*.[3] Accordingly, the contemporary central message of both Diakonia and Caritas Theory is a reflection on the church's charitable praxis, which is synonymous to social welfare services by the church.

Suffice it to mention that those who first spoke of diakonia were not the linguists or theologians of nowadays. According to John Collins[4] and Kari Latvus,[5] the term was formally introduced by Lutheran churchmen of nineteenth-century Germany, who sought to establish a form of Christian ministry among the displaced, delinquent, sick, poor, illiterate, and all those affected by the aftermath of the Napoleonic wars and onset of industrialization. Up until the first decades of the nineteenth century the term was still absent from the church circles and broader society. It was during a conference organized by King Friedrich Wilhelm IV of Prussia in Monbijou Castle on the relations of church and state held in 1856 (November 2–December 5) that the term diakonia was officially adopted as a fixed concept for referring to ideas, theology, and practical work among the poor. The conference was intended to solve the question regarding the diaconate (office of the deacon) of the church, but ironically and practically ended up introducing the caritative concept of Diakonia.[6]

The original Greek meaning for "diakonia" applies to a number of meanings from ministry, service, helps and services of various kinds, which can range in meaning from "spiritual" biblical teaching (Acts 6:4) to the "practical" giving of provisions, supplies, support, and finances to those in need (e.g., 2 Cor 9:12).[7] Accordingly, *diakonos*, a derivative of diakonia,

---

2. Garcia-Irons, *Place of Spirituality*, 1–7.
3. Opatrný, "Caritas Theory," 301; Šimr, "Diakonia in the Public Sphere," 154–60.
4. Collins, *Diakonia*, 8.
5. Latvus, *Diaconia as Care for the Poor*, 83.
6. Latvus, *Diaconia as Care for the Poor*, 84.
7. Goodrick and Kohlenberger, *NIV Exhaustive Concordance*, 1326.

means "servant, minister, a person who renders service and helps to others, in some contexts with an implication of lower status." The same Greek word is also transliterated as "deacon", meaning a trusted officer of helps and services in the local church. That is why, Hermann Beyer,[8] in his legendary influential article in Kittel's *Theological Dictionary of the New Testament* argues that diakonia in the New Testament means both "'waiting at table" or in a rather wider sense "provision for bodily sustenance'" and also any other "discharge of service" in genuine love, which is also translated as charity.

*Charity* is the King James Version (KJV) Bible translation of the Greek word *agape*,[9] which according to Edward Goodrick and John Kohlenberger III's NIV Exhaustive Concordance usually refers to God's active love for his Son Jesus Christ and people, as well as the love that God's people are to have for him, each other, and even their enemies.[10] James Douglas and Merrill Tenney also write that charity represents the Latin word *caritas*, which in the Vulgate (the principal Latin version of the Bible) is found in the passages where the KJV has the word love.[11] The just cited co-authors further comment that charity in the Bible never means necessarily giving to the poor, but always refers to a God-given love that includes respect and concern for the one loved, a concept that seems to be overwhelmingly implied in 1 Corinthians 13 as highlighted in verse 3 as follows.

> And though I bestow all my goods to feed the poor, and though I give my body to be burned, and have not charity, it profiteth me nothing. (1 Cor 13:3 KJV)

Seen from the perspective of "respect and concern for the one loved," which James Douglas and Merrill Tenney refer to, it rather appears that charity bestows certain ethical obligations on philanthropy than negate it.[12] This observation is supported by the wider context of the Christian Scripture, which teaches that acts of philanthropy, especially such as done to the poor, are vital Christian virtues. For example, Matthew 25:35–40 reads as follows:

> "For I was hungry and you gave me food, I was thirsty and you gave me drink, I was a stranger and you welcomed me, I was naked

---

8. Beyer, "Diakonew, Diakonia, Diakonos," 10.
9. Douglas and Tenney, *New International Dictionary*, 200.
10. Goodrick and Kohlenberger, *NIV Exhaustive Concordance*, 1524.
11. Douglas and Tenney, *New International Dictionary*, 200.
12. Douglas and Tenney, *New International Dictionary*, 200.

and you clothed me, I was sick and you visited me, I was in prison and you came to me." Then the righteous will then answer him, "Lord, when did we see thee hungry and feed thee, or thirsty and give thee drink? And when did we see thee a stranger and welcomed thee, or naked and clothe thee? And when did we see thee sick or in prison and visit thee?" And the King will answer them, "Truly, I say to you, as you did it to one of the least of these my brethren, you did it to me." (Matt 25:35–40 RSV)

According to the "Greek-English lexicon of the New Testament based on semantic domains" by Johannes Louw and Eugene Nida,[13] the original Greek for the phrase, "the least" as found in verse 40 is *tón elachíston* and means, "pertaining to the lowest status, lowest, least important, last." Commenting on the same phrase, the New Matthew Henry Commentary edited by Martin Manser[14] records that just as Christ makes the most of the disciple's physical works of mercy, even so he makes the best of the weaknesses of the poor and needy, even those considered to be least important. The just quoted source further states that "what is rewarded here is the relieving of the poor for Christ's sake" and the good acts of kindness done in the name of the Lord will, therefore, be acceptable. Said another way, social welfare services done out of love in the name of the Lord are hereby encouraged and will be rewarded.

As such, Paul's words in 1 Corinthians 13:3 with regard to charity should not be misconstrued to negate acts of philanthropy such as social welfare to alleviate the plight of the poor. For instance, in the same context (1 Cor 13:1–2) he speaks of the gifts of tongues, prophecy, and faith as amounting to "nothing" without charity, certainly not to render these grace gifts nothingness, but to rather emphasize that they need to be qualified by charity. In like manner, giving in this case should emanate from a charitable attitude of respect and concern for the recipient if it has to be ethically acceptable. The words of Pope Benedict XVI best lay this argument on the line when he states that "human beings always need something more than technically proper care. They need humanity. They need heartfelt concern."[15] This is akin to one of the core principles of traditional African philosophy commonly known as "Ubuntu" (humanness), which is well expressed through a South African Xhosa tribe saying, "Umntu ungumntu

---

13. Louw and Nida, *Indices*, 7.
14. Manser, *New Matthew Henry Commentary*, 1537.
15. Benedict XVI, *Deus Caritas Est*, 31.

ngabanye abantu [a person is a person through other persons]."[16] From this point of view, it can be inferred that charity bestows critical ethical aspects on philanthropic strategies such as respect, humaneness, and heartfelt concern for the recipients of charitable acts.

From the foregoing discourse, it can be deduced that the concepts of charity and charitable purpose evolve from a theological background and, according to Karel Šimr,[17] can also be discovered within the pastoral (or practical) theological theories. In her article on "Church in the Mission of Christ," Annette Noller writes that current practical theological theories argue that diaconal enterprises and diaconal engagement can be seen as a special dimension of the church in which the gospel of God's redeeming grace is communicated as charity.[18] According to the just cited author, sociological theories such as systems theories have also inspired practical theologians to think about church and diakonia in innovative ways. Clear linkages are thus perceived among charity, social work, and practical theology. As such, any meaningful ethical evaluation of philanthropic strategies implemented by charitable organizations should consider perspectives from these disciplines as well.

Before going on to formulate the theoretical framework for the ethical evaluating of philanthropic strategies employed by charitable organizations, it is necessary to define charitable organizations and also identify the types of charitable organizations that are operational in remote African communities such as Mongu district of Western Zambia.

## DEFINING CHARITABLE ORGANIZATIONS

Global experiences of defining charitable organizations can be a problematic process, but the global experiences can, however, be of help towards a local definition of charitable organizations.[19] The just cited source in the footnote reckons that the meaning of charitable organizations and charitable purposes is not defined in statutes, but at common law.[20] As it were, the common law definition of charity and charitable purposes is mainly based

16. Wet, *Understanding Transformational Development*, 28.
17. Šimr, "Diakonia in the Public Sphere," 154.
18. Noller, "Church in the Mission of Jesus Christ," 49.
19. Treasury, *Definition of Charity*, 3.
20. Common law is the part of English law that is derived from custom and judicial precedent rather than statutes. See Chen, "Common Law."

on the Preamble to the Statute of Charitable Uses enacted by the English Parliament in 1601 (also known as the Statute of Elizabeth) and the historic case of the Commissioners for Special Purposes of Income Tax v Pemsel (also known as Pemsel's Case),[21] which classified charitable organizations into four categories in connection with the following headings:

i. Relief of poverty,

ii. Advancement of education,

iii. Advancement of religion, and

iv. Other purposes beneficial to the community not falling under any of the preceding categories.

As per Pemsel's Case, any common law definition of charity requires that a charity has a charitable purpose and be for the benefit of the public.[22] Several other scholars agree with the foregoing categorical definition of charitable organizations.[23] For instance, the Zambian government's definition of a charity, which is synonymous to an NGO, as cited in the introduction, to a greater extent also adheres to the Pemsel Case criteria of charity and charitable purposes.

Suffice it to highlight also that there have been several attempts for alternative definitions of charity. According to a publication by Matthew Harding and others titled *Defining Charity: A Literature Review*,[24] the most successful attempt in recent years in this regard has been to divide the term charity into two forms, namely, separation of charitable status in trust law from charitable status in taxation law (division by policy function); and the creation of a hierarchy of charities. This approach seems to stem from Nigel Gravells' long held view of the validation of the purpose of public trusts and is supported by other renowned commentators on the subject of charity such as Susan Bright, Nuzhat Malik, and Gino Dal Pont.[25] Notwithstanding the grounds for this argument, the mainstream view, however, seems to be that it would not be manifestly convenient to have a division of charity

21. Halsbury et al., *Commissioners v. Pemsel*, 5.

22. Martin, "Legal Concept of Charity," 20.

23. Bourgeois, *Law of Charitable and Not-for-Profit*, 9; Harding et al., *Defining Charity*, 6; Hoque and Parker, *Performance Management*, 288; Swarbrick, "Income Tax."

24. Harding et al., *Defining Charity*, 19–20.

25. See Gravell, "Public Purpose Trusts," 397; Bright, "Charity and Trusts," 36–37; Malik, "Defining 'Charity' and 'Charitable Purposes'"; Dal Pont, "Why Define Charity?," 5–37.

law for various reasons such as duplicity, complexity, and incongruence from the very nature of the categories themselves as Harding and others observe.[26] For instance, the just cited co-authors further write that the taxation law is already implicit in the trust law as the content of charity also helps to determine the level of public benefit that justifies tax expenditure. From this perspective, all charities ought to be treated alike as much as possible.

The second and less influential approach has been to divide charities into a hierarchy, with the top priority given to charities that help the disadvantaged. Although this argument has hitherto not garnered much influence, it has also been supported by renowned figures such as Michael Gousmett and Prince Philip the Duke of Edinburgh,[27] who propose that highest tax relief should be given to humanitarian causes, while less relief should be offered for both community and environmental benefit.

In view of the foregoing global attempts to define charities and some of the adopted definitions such as that of my country—Zambia, an ethical evaluation of charitable organizations operating in African communities would mainly be based on the definitive criteria used in Pemsel's Case of 1891.[28] Michael Gousmett also writes that the four principal divisions of charitable purpose in Pemsel's Case of 1891 have been the key criteria against which charitable activity is measured.[29]

## Types of Charitable Organizations

To rightly categorise charitable organizations, we need to look at the different functions that they perform and the sectors they support. For the purpose of clear understanding, charitable organizations in this book have been divided into seven categories based on their inclusion in the common law definition and in accordance with respective current issues with charities.[30] Suffice it to mention that most of these categories could still be broken down further as may be necessary to find more specific charity types.

---

26. Harding et al., *Defining Charity*, 20.
27. See Harding et al., *Defining Charity*, 20.
28. Halsbury et al., *Commissioners v. Pemsel*, 5.
29. Gousmett, *Modernizing Charity Law*, 23.
30. Ascot Day Centre, "Six Types of Charitable Organizations"; Nexus Marketing, "Types of Charities"; Vodo, *Faith-Based Organizations*.

The seven charity categories identified for this publication are hereafter explained in no particular order.

*Educational Charities*

As enshrined in the Statute of Elizabeth of 1601, one of the key roles of charities is the advancement of education. Educational charities help students whose financial background cannot sustain them in school or those who, by virtue of their outstanding performances or aptitude, deserve scholarship in one way or another.[31] The just cited source in the footnote writes that some charities donate funds to different schools while others prefer to set up their own schools where they educate and support all the students they identify as deserving such help. The assistance can be in form of scholarships, provision of learning materials and financial aid, and such support as may be deemed appropriate can be given to students or through their parents, guardians, or respective school administrative offices.

Examples of educational charities in Africa and Zambia are *UNICEF* and *Keeping Girls in School*, respectively.

*Faith-Based Organizations (FBOs)*

Faith-based organizations such as Christian organizations are increasingly becoming important in the provision of social and welfare services of many states and communities through the voluntary sector. Just as Teuta Vodo[32] also writes, FBOs meet a wide range of community needs and fill in the gap between the demand for and supply of welfare provisions. In addition, they continue to exert political and social impact. Most of the charitable organizations operating among African communities can be classified as FBOs (e.g., World Vision International, Catholic Relief Services, Action Aid, Caritas, etc.).

*Health Charities*

Health charities aim to assist sick people and those with physical disabilities to have access to quality health care services as included in The Charities

---

31. Nexus Marketing, "Types of Charities."
32. Vodo, *Faith-Based Organizations*, 2.

Act of 2006 for England and Wales, which is essentially an expansion of the four heads of charities revealed in Pemsel's Case of 1891.[33] Accordingly, the assistance can take many forms including providing funds for medical research, promotion of health awareness, and paying accumulated hospital bills for those who have difficulties in raising the required funds.[34]

Some examples of health charities working in Africa are the World Health Organization, Center for Disease Control, and Center for Infectious Diseases Research in Zambia.

## Art and Culture Charities

The central focus of this type of charities is the protection and preservation of cultural heritage and art.[35] Such charities as these may also be further classified into Museum and Art Galleries and Historical Societies for the preservation of such art and cultural heritage.

As at the writing of this book, the government of the Republic of Zambia was working together with the Barotse Royal Establishment through the National Heritage Conservation Commission to secure enlisting of the Barotse Floodplain on the UNESCO World Heritage List as World Heritage Cultural Landscape.[36] Whether UNESCO and its cooperating partners will or have charitable uses and purposes for the prospective world heritage cultural landscape or not, is an ethical question.

## Environment Charities

These charities focus on environmental preservation, sustenance, and development.[37] They are the type of charities that champion the use of greener and renewable energy sources campaign, environmental conservation and protection of the ecosystem.

---

33. Proirier, *Charity Law in New Zealand*, 87.
34. Ascot Day Centre, "Six Types of Charitable Organizations."
35. Ascot Day Centre, "Six Types of Charitable Organizations."
36. MT Zambia, *Application for Inscription of Barotse Plains*.
37. Proirier, *Charity Law in New Zealand*, 87.

## Wildlife Conservation Charities

These charities raise funds for use in wildlife conservation and the protection of pets and other animals' wellbeing.[38] As such, any person who is willing to contribute to animal welfare can do so through animal charities established for that purpose.

As an example, a non-profit making conservation organization known as African Parks is co-managing one of the largest and oldest national parks in Africa that dates back to the nineteenth century—the Liuwa Plain National Park in Western Zambia—in partnership with the Department of National Parks and Wildlife (DNPW) and the native Barotse Royal Establishment since 2003.[39] Again, whether this is absolute altruism by the African Parks or not, is an ethical question.

## International NGOs

International NGOs are big charities with headquarters in one country (usually in a developed country), but with branches in various other countries around the world. These types of charitable organizations also have their presence among poor African communities where they operate. The same ethical question of charitable uses and purposes alluded to the previous sections resonates herein as well as it also influences the ethical thought of this book.

Suffice it to mention that new charities emerge from time to time and some of them can fall into or out of some of the foregoing categories based on their agenda. The point is that classification of charities is dynamic and ever-changing with time and space.[40] As such, there is need for continuous update on the trending types of charities.

## Charitable Organizations Prevalent among African Communities

Regarding the work of this book, I will focus particularly on an ethical evaluation of philanthropic strategies of international NGOs and FBOs because they are the most sort of charitable organizations operating among African communities such as Mongu district and Zambia as a country. For ethical

---

38. Proirier, *Charity Law in New Zealand*, 87.
39. African Parks, "Liuwa Plain."
40. Ascot Day Centre, "Six Types of Charitable Organizations."

reasons, I have withheld the respective names of NGOs that I evaluated in my study.

## Operationalization Perspectives

This chapter has dealt with the operationalization of charitable organizations operating among poor African communities such as Mongu in Western Zambia. Accordingly, we have explored in details the aspects of charity and charitable organizations, and identified the types of charitable organizations prevalent among African communities.

As it were, the word *"charity"* has got its roots in the Bible and it underlines the idea of *diakonia* in Protestant theology, while in Catholic theology it embraces the *caritas theory*. The contemporary central message of both diakonia and caritas theory is a reflection on the church's charitable praxis, which is synonymous to social welfare services by the church. Somewhere in the mid-1800s, establishments called charitable organizations were set up in England and they consisted of church personnel and volunteers who were designated to help to the poor, homeless, and severely ill people in society. The principles underlying those early social work practices were founded on the biblical idea of charity.

The meaning of charitable organizations and charitable purposes is not defined in statutes, but at common law and the common law definition is mainly based on the Preamble to the Statute of Charitable Uses enacted by the English Parliament in 1601 (also known as the Statute of Elizabeth) and Commissioners for Special Purposes of Income Tax v Pemsel (Pemsel's Case ). As per Pemsel's Case, any common law definition of charity should require of a charity to have a charitable purpose and be for the benefit of the public. The four principal divisions of charitable purpose in Pemsel's Case of 1891 have been the key criteria against which charitable activities are measured. For example, the Zambian government's definition of a charity, which is synonymous to an NGO, to a greater extent also adheres to Pemsel's Case criteria of charitable purpose.

Finally, to rightly categorise charitable organizations, one needs to look at the different functions that they perform and the sectors they support. The most types of charitable organizations found in Zambia and Africa have been identified as international NGOs and FBOs.

In the next chapter, we will discover, through literature survey in the broader spectrum, the theoretical framework for the ethical evaluation of philanthropic strategies employed by charitable organisations.

# 3

# Literature Survey

## INTRODUCTION

The purpose of this chapter is to critically analyze key aspects of the subject under investigation in order to establish the meta-theoretical assumptions informing the work of this book, as well as to cast new insight into the subject matter. This is in accordance with the purpose of literature research in academia.[1] As Christa Delport and Christa Fouché also write, a researcher or an author should endeavor to learn how other scholars have theorized and conceptualized similar subjects, what they have empirically found, which methods they have used, and what effects these aspects have had on their respective works.[2]

In view of the foregoing rationale, theoretical considerations in this chapter will focus on the historical development of charity law and theoretical framework for the evaluation of philanthropic strategies employed by charitable organizations.

## HISTORICAL DEVELOPMENT OF CHARITY LAW

The meanings of charitable organization and charitable purpose have so far been attributed to common law, but common law itself as applied in England and other countries that have adopted it, such as Zambia, cannot be understood without knowledge of its historical development. As Donald

---

1. Kritzinger, *Navorsing in die Fakulteit Teologie*, 16; Osmer, *Practical Theology*, 48.
2. Delport and Fouché, "Place of Theory," 263.

Proirier writes, common law is the accumulation over time of decisions made by judges and these decisions are usually linked to facts that have gained their meaning from the social and economic situations of the time when they were decided.[3] Accordingly, the current definition of charity and charitable purpose is based on over four hundred years of common law according to Treasury of The Australian Government[4] and other reliable sources. As such, it is important to understand the historical background from which this law has evolved in order to comprehend and apply it appropriately.

History has it that during the sixteenth century, the English society saw that the role of the church in charitable work was declining and it was increasingly recognized during the reign of Queen Elizabeth I that poverty was a national problem.[5] Happening about the same time were also series of catastrophic events that exacerbated the situation and these included multiple disastrous harvests, the Spanish war, high inflation, domestic and international economic depressions, and the Black Death or bubonic plague which killed about 14 percent of London's population.[6] As one would fearfully anticipate, these events led to widespread poverty, unemployment and vagrancy. In his article titled, "1601 Preamble: The State's Agenda for Charity," Blake Bromley records that the English state under Elizabeth I at that time intervened and established workhouses to discipline and make productive the poor who could work and required of local parishes to provide for their own poor.[7]

Due to its own lack of funds to alleviate the desperate situation of its citizens, the English state then turned to the encouragement of private philanthropy to assist, and this was done through three major avenues.[8] First, the Court of Chancery was reinforced as the dominant legal mechanism for enforcing charitable purposes. Second, the privileges that the law provided to charitable institutions, including fixing many technical defects and ensuring that they did not fail due to uncertainty, were confirmed and

---

3. Proirier, *Charity Law in New Zealand*, 78.
4. Treasury, *Definition of Charity*, 1.
5. Martin, "Legal Concept of Charity," 20.
6. Bromley, "1601 Preamble," 50–78; Brundage, *English Poor Laws*; Glatter and Finkelman, "History of the Plague," 176–77; McGregor-Lowndes, "Diversions of Charitable Assets," 4–5.
7. Bromley, "1601 Preamble," 198–200.
8. Chesterman, "Charities, Trusts," 24–28; Martin, "Legal Concept of Charity," 21.

## Literature Survey

enhanced. Third, the Statute of Charitable Uses 1601, commonly referred to as *The Statute of Elizabeth*, was enacted. The aim of this statute was to appoint the bishop of a diocese and the local gentry as commissioners to supervise the administration of most charities and to prevent any misuse of charitable property. As Fiona Martin, senior lecturer in the Australian School of Business at the University of New South Wales, writes, the commissioners were empowered to provide checks and balances such as inquiring into abuses and breaches of trusts, negligence, misemployments, defrauding, or misgovernment of any property given for such charitable and godly uses as listed in the statute's preamble.[9]

According to William Kitchener Jordan and The Institute of Chartered Accountants of India, the Statute of Charitable Uses 1601 did not actually create a new concept of charitable purposes but rather codified a body of law that was just really a classical statement.[10] The later of the two just cited sources further states that the statute has since been interpreted and expanded in a considerable body of case law within and outside England, Zambia inclusive. David Swarbrick provides a long list of case laws that have cited the Statute of Charitable Uses 1601 right up to the current year of his publication (2020), which also happens to be the same year that the research for this book was being conducted.[11] The Charities Act of 2006 for England and Wales expanded the four heads of charitable purposes to thirteen categories as follows:[12]

i. The prevention or relief of poverty.

ii. The advancement of education.

iii. The advancement of religion.

iv. The advancement of health or the saving of lives.

v. The advancement of citizenship or community development.

vi. The advancement of the arts, culture, heritage or science.

vii. The advancement of amateur sport.

---

9. Martin, "Legal Concept of Charity," 21.

10. See Martin, "Legal Concept of Charity," 22; ICAI, *Study on Laws Governing Charitable Organisations*, 10.

11. Swarbrick, "Income Tax Special Commissioners v. Pemsel."

12. Proirier, *Charity Law in New Zealand*, 87.

viii. The advancement of human rights, conflict resolution or reconciliation or the promotion of religious or racial harmony or equality and diversity.

ix. The advancement of environmental protection or improvement.

x. The relief of those in need by reason of youth, age, ill-health, disability, financial hardship or other disability.

xi. The advancement of animal welfare.

xii. The promotion of the efficiency of the armed forces of the Crown, or the efficiency of the police, fire and rescue services or ambulance services.

xiii. Any other purpose recognized as charitable under existing charity law, analogous to, or within the spirit of, any purposes listed above or analogous to, or within the spirit of, any purposes recognized under charity law as falling within the above categories.

With regard to the foregoing discourse, Donald Proirier writes that the development of the welfare state is probably the most influential social factor on philanthropy and legislation pertaining to charity law in modern time.[13]

It is the evolution of charity law around the Statute of Charitable Uses 1601 that is important for the framework of this book too. According to James Fishman, the statute unintentionally created a definition of charity and charitable purpose that resonates in charity law to date.[14] The most important feature of this piece of legislation is that it set out a preamble that comprehensively listed for the first time a range of charitable purposes, which has also been confirmed in subsequent case law as the foundation of the modern legal definition of charity and charitable purpose.[15] As such, the ethical evaluation of philanthropic strategies implemented by charitable organizations operating in Africa should also be guided by the framework established within the evolution of charity law around the Statute of Charitable Uses 1601.

---

13. Proirier, *Charity Law in New Zealand*, 85.
14. Fishman, "Political Use of Private Benevolence."
15. Proirier, *Charity Law in New Zealand*, 85.

Literature Survey

## THEORETICAL FRAMEWORK FOR THE ETHICAL EVALUATION OF PHILANTHROPIC STRATEGIES BY CHARITABLE ORGANIZATIONS

In view of the discourses of the preceding sections and chapters, the theoretical framework for the ethical evaluation of philanthropic strategies by charitable organizations operating in Africa will be based on an interdisciplinary perspective of theological and sociological discourses comprising pastoral theology, social work, and common law. For the sake of better understanding, an explication of these disciplines and concepts and how they interlink within the discourse of charity and charitable purposes is hereafter provided.

### Ethical Perspectives from Pastoral Theology

So far it has been established that the concepts of "charity" and "charitable purpose" evolve from a theological background and can be located within the pastoral or practical theological theory. As Don Browning positively argues, the dialogue of practical theology is not restricted to the Christian community and sources as it involves critical reflection on the church's dialogue with Christian sources and other communities of experience and interpretation in order to guide its action toward holistic transformation.[16] Among others, practical theology engages constructively with relevant disciplines of neighboring social sciences such as sociology, anthropology, and psychology.[17] This is also affirmed by the interplay of pastoral theology, social work, and common law in the theoretical framework for the subject under study in this book.

One of the most important focal concepts of pastoral theology is an augmented holistic evolution of the quality of life of the local people through responsible interaction with the created order to the glory of God.[18] Wagner Kuhn[19] of Andrews University also reckons that the importance of this concept lies in the fact that holistic transformation of the individual and community is the ultimate goal of Christian education and development.

---

16. Browning, *Fundamental Practical Theology*, 36.
17. Opatrný, "Caritas Theory," 306–7.
18. Bosch, *Transforming Mission*, 385; Louw, *Interculturality and Wholeness*, 25; Osmer, *Practical Theology*, 5–6; Samuel and Sugden, *Mission as Transformation*, 38.
19. Kuhn, *Need for a Biblical Theology*, 106–7.

Within pastoral theology, the concepts of diakonia and caritas theory underpin philanthropic strategies by charitable organizations from a multi-disciplinary perspective. For instance, Michal Opatrný, in his article titled "Caritas Theory as Theological Discourse within Education in Social Work," argues that caritas theory was originally not a purely theological reflection on the praxis of charity, but a multi-disciplinary reflection on charitable work.[20] He bases his argument on the works of other renowned scholars in the field such as Ernst Engelke, who clearly argues that caritas theory was founded for the scholarly support of charity and as a mediator between theology and social work.[21] Similarly, the Protestant view of this concept presented as diakonia is also an academic discipline in the form of an interdisciplinary theoretical reflection on diaconal praxis within the areas of healthcare, social work, and education, whether at the level of a local congregation or professional social institution as Kjell Nordstokke writes.[22] To buttress his point, he makes reference to one of the most important international documents on diakonia completed by the Lutheran World Federation titled, *Diakonia in Context: Transformation, Reconciliation, Empowerment*.[23] Accordingly, the cited document states that diakonia is a theological concept that points to the very identity and mission of the church and a call to action in response to challenges of human suffering, injustice, and care for creation.

Drawing on the works of Don Browning and Paul Ricoeur—some of the most eminent American practical theologians so far—Richard Osmer also highlights some important ethical aspects in practical theology, which also contribute to the theoretical framework for the topic under study in this book as hereafter outlined.[24]

### Ethical Reflection with Universal Ethical Principles

This is particularly important because it allows moral communities to test their present practices against universally accepted ethical principles. For instance, Osmer poses important questions in this regard as follows:

20. Opatrný, "Caritas Theory," 302.
21. See Engelke, *Wissenschaft Soziale Arbeit*.
22. Nordstokke, "Study of Diakonia," 171.
23. Nordstokke, *Diakonia in Context*, 8.
24. See Browning, *Fundamental Practical Theology*; Ricoeur, *Oneself as Another*; Osmer, *Practical Theology*, 147–53.

i. Do these moral communities regard the moral worth of others as equal to their own?

ii. When the interests of their community conflict with the interests of others, are they committed to procedures that are fair and open to all parties?

iii. Can they enter sympathetically into the perspectives of groups that are different from themselves?[25]

As Osmer observes, human beings are likely to put interests of their families and immediate communities above those of all other people, especially in situations of moral conflict and dire need. Therefore, ethical tests such as these are important also for the ethical evaluation of philanthropic strategies applied by charitable organization such as operate among poor African communities. Don Browning also adds that the application of ethical norms should not only occur at the end of a process but ought to be present from the outset and influence it throughout.[26]

## Equal Regard

There is an ethic of equal regard grounded in the narratives of creation and the ministry of Christ that points to the inherent dignity and worth of all human beings as Richard Osmer writes.[27] He adds that Christian love, which is herein referred to as charity, should also be understood and expressed in an ethic of equal regard. Osmer further writes that in the creation narratives, human beings are portrayed as being created in the image of God and are, therefore, worthy of respect in personal relationships and fair treatment in social institutions. In the narratives of Christ's ministry, he (Christ) is cited telling his disciples at least eight times that they ought to love their neighbours as themselves and follow the golden rule—do to others what you would like them to do to you. Osmer concludes his section on ethical interpretation by stating that general principles like equal regard and love, as well as other concrete guidelines and rules, can help us to understand and address the moral issues at stake in episodes, situations, and contexts.[28] This framework also forms general norms and principles that

25. Osmer, *Practical Theology*, 149–50.
26. Browning, *Fundamental Practical Theology*, 39.
27. Osmer, *Practical Theology*, 151.
28. Osmer, *Practical Theology*, 152.

may be applied to the subject hereby under study as well as the criteria for selection or goals that can be attained by an acceptable alternative.

## Good Practice

A third approach to ethics from pastoral theology is good practice, which provides ethical guidance in two ways.[29] First, it offers models of good practice, either from the past or present, which can be employed to reform present praxis. Second, good practice can generate new understandings of God, the Christian life, and social values beyond those provided by the received traditions. Accordingly, observing good practice in other organizations is a powerful source of ethical guidance.

Alongside the role of good practice is present practice, which is the generative source of new understandings of God, the Christian life, and social values. As such good practice is more than just a model; it is epistemic. Therefore, good practice also finds relevance for the ethical evaluation of philanthropic strategies employed by charitable organizations operating among poor African communities such as remote areas of Zambia.

## Practical Moral Reasoning (Phronesis)

Practical moral reasoning is necessary for the application of moral principles and commitment to particular situations.[30] The concept stems from the Greek word transliterated as *phronesis*, which literally means "wisdom, understanding" according to Edward Goodrick and John Kohlenberger III's NIV exhaustive concordance.[31] In the context of practical theological ethics, phronesis implies practical wisdom derived from learning and evidence of practical things, just as the Oxford Encyclopedia of Terms records.[32] According to the just cited source, phronesis leads to breakthrough in thinking and creativity and enables an individual to discern and make judgments about what is the right thing to do in a particular situation and how to do it.

---

29. Osmer, *Practical Theology*, 152–53.
30. Osmer, *Practical Theology*, 149.
31. Goodrick and Kohlenberger, *NIV Exhaustive Concordance*, 1601.
32. Oxford Review, "Phronesis."

This may be seen as similar to, but is definitely not the same as, ethical reflection. Whereas ethical reflection involves reflection with universal ethical principles, in phronesis, "the meaning of any universal, or any norm, is only justified and determined in and through its concretisation."[33] Accordingly, practical moral reasoning in this sense is knowledge of what to do or how to act in a particular situation and involves understanding what is at stake in that situation. As such, it is not merely the virtue of making the right technical decision to get the right end in a given circumstance; it is about reflecting on both the means and end at stake in any decision and action. To lay it on the line, it is first and foremost a mode of ethical reasoning, which is akin to making ethical decisions.

With regard to the topic hereby under investigation, practical moral reasoning is particularly important in evaluating the means and application of moral principles in philanthropy because it is not true that the end always justifies the means.

*Summary of Ethical Perspectives from Pastoral Theology*

The concepts of "charity" and "charitable purpose" evolve from a theological background and can be located within the pastoral theological theory, which embraces applied theology in Catholic theology and practical theology in the Protestant theological discourse. The dialogue of pastoral theology is, however, not restricted to the Christian community and sources, but involves critical reflection on the church's dialogue with Christian sources and other communities of experience and interpretation so as to guide the church's action toward holistic transformation. As such, it has been deductively inferred that the framework for the subject under study comprises pastoral theology, social work, and common law. Accordingly, the ethical perspectives from pastoral theology with regard to the topic under study comprise ethical reflection with universal ethical principles, equal regard, good practice, and practical moral reasoning.

Next are ethical perspectives from the field of social work.

---

33. Shapcott, "Phronesis, Ethics, and Realism."

## Ethical Perspectives from Social Work

The International Federation of Social Workers defines social work as a practice-based profession and an academic discipline that promotes social change and development, social cohesion, and the empowerment and liberation of people.[34] Accordingly, principles of social justice, human rights, collective responsibility and respect for diversities underpin the practice of social work. The discourse of social work is also enriched significantly by theological ethics through the latter's emphatic criticism of the limited focus of professional ethics of social work, which focus mainly on deontological and utilitarian ethics.[35] This is to imply that the ethical perspectives from pastoral theology as discussed in the previous section also apply to the discourse of social work.

It is also important to mention that the issue of ethics in social work is not easy to reconcile globally because the conceptions of social work and social policy differ from one state to another, which is customary in the discourse of social work.[36] In social work, ethics reflect the profession's guiding philosophy of advancing human welfare and its commitment to ensure that social workers everywhere are strongly united with common belief systems. Therefore, despite the varying nature of social ethics geographically, culturally, and politically, it is generally accepted that ethics in social work can be summed up into six fundamental foci, which Henry Ajibo,[37] a lecturer of social work in public health at the University of Nigeria succinctly outlines as follows:

i. **Social justice**: represents fairness in the distribution of resources and opportunities to all. It manifests through challenging negative discrimination, recognizing diversity, distributing resources equitably, and challenging unjust policies and practices.

ii. **Service**: at all times, the social worker must be ready to serve every person with his or her knowledge and skills, except where restrained by professional ethics.

---

34. IFSW, "Global Definition of Social Work."
35. Opatrný, "Caritas Theory," 306–7; Šrajer, "Etika a Požadavek," 81–88.
36. Opatrný, "Caritas Theory," 303.
37. Ajibo, *Values, Ethics*, 32–33.

iii. **Dignity and worth of the human person:** everyone is entitled to his or her full respect regardless of appearance, religion, gender, social status, race, tribe, etc.

iv. **Integrity:** social workers hold honesty and truthfulness as strong virtues.

v. **Importance of human relationships:** everyone is important as much as human relationships in themselves are very strong resources in problem solving.

vi. **Competence:** social workers should know the limits of their expertise and are bound to refer cases appropriately in such contexts as might require services of other experts in the field.

Suffice it to mention that the foregoing outlined ethical considerations are also directly applicable to ethics in charity. For instance, by default the discourse of charity works also requires social justice as well as respect for the dignity and worth of the human person.

## Spirituality in Social work and Social Work Ethics

Numerous studies so far indicate that there is a historical connection between spirituality and social work.[38] It is, however, of prior necessity to critically distinguish between spirituality in the theological sense and spirituality in the sense of social sciences in order to have a better understanding of this related sub-topic and how it fits into the wider context of the discourse of this book. Despite the difficult in distinguishing between the two, what is clear first of all is that spirituality is closely connected with theology, but not exclusively contained by it.[39]

In traditional Western theology, spirituality has been subjected to the dominance and interiorization of the contents of dogmatics and morality.[40] For instance, Edna Lezotte writes that in Protestant theological tradition, spirituality is usually referred to as devotion or piety, while Roman Catholicism thinks of spirituality as one's distinctive way of following Christ,

---

38. Canda and Furman, *Spiritual Diversity in Social Work*; Erikson, *Identity*; Fowler, *Stages of Faith*; Garcia-Irons, *Place of Spirituality*; Lezotte, "Spirituality and Social Work"; Loue, *Social Work Values*.

39. King, *Search for Spirituality*; Niekerk, "Spirituality and Religion," 10.

40. Villiers, "Spirituality, Theology," 104; Hoogen, "Spirituality," 2.

communing with God, and growing in the life of faith.[41] Lezotte further writes that in modern Orthodox tradition, spirituality has come to refer to a person's life and activity in relationship to God, oneself, other people, and all things in reference to God. In a possible summative form, Jochen Hardt and others are of the view that spirituality has four main components or dimensions, namely belief in God, engaging in a search for meaning, mindfulness, and a feeling of security.[42]

Traditional Western theology is, nevertheless, criticized for having lost its dynamic transformative nature and for indulging in debates about irrelevant dogmatic or exegetical intricacies as Robert Solomon, a distinguished teaching professor of business and philosophy at the University of Texas, writes.[43] Pieter de Villiers, a research fellow and professor extraordinarius in biblical spirituality at the University of the Free State, also observes that such a proposition seems to be rigid and in conflict with the critical mind as influenced by the Socratic principle of discovering truth through analytical and dialectical dialogue.[44]

Since the late twentieth century, however, there has been a notable change within theology in a movement best described as contextual theologies as Pieter de Villiers also writes.[45] According to the just cited author and others such as Toine van den Hoogen and Diana Villegas, a theological definition of spirituality should involve purposeful approaches to the living of a life guided by beliefs deemed to address questions of meaning and to make possible greater wholeness and transcendence.[46] Just as the Australian public intellectual, writer, and interdisciplinary scholar David Tacey also writes, from a theological perspective spirituality is about personal empowerment, but it is not private because out this empowerment will flow political and social transformation.[47] This seems to be a more promising avenue towards addressing the critique on the rigidity and controversially limited focus of traditional Western theological view of spirituality.

In the perspective of social sciences, however, spirituality encompasses a much broader spectrum of humanity in relation to both the tangible

---

41. Lezotte, "Spirituality and Social Work," 2.
42. Hardt et al., "Spirituality Questionnaire," 116–22.
43. Solomon, *Spiritualiteit voor Sceptici*, 46.
44. Villiers, "Spirituality, Theology," 99–100.
45. Villiers, "Spirituality, Theology," 105.
46. See Hoogen, "Spirituality," 2; Villegas, "Spirituality and Belief," 2–8.
47. Tacey, *Spirituality Revolution*, 66.

and intangible worlds.[48] For instance, from the perspective of psychology of religion, Daniela Vilani and others write that spirituality is the human desire for transcendence, introspection, interconnectedness, and the quest for meaning in life, and this appears to be same for all humans regardless of their religious statuses.[49] According to the American Sociological Association, spirituality in sociology of religion can be defined as individual and group efforts to find meaning for existence within or outside of organized religion.[50] Hence Christopher Tirkey sees spirituality in this regard as a diverse concept existing among all of humanity.[51] The just cited author and renowned scholar on Indian religions argues that there is not one uniform concept or experience of spirituality because humans have different cultural and religious backgrounds, different socio-economic and political situations, and varied psychological conditionings, all of which contribute to the plurality and diversity of spiritualities.

The role played by spirituality in social work cannot be over-emphasized, as every person wants to believe in something intrinsic or extrinsic.[52] To that end, human spirituality manifests itself in different forms even outside social work. For example, Gus Speth, a United States of America advisor on climate change once said, "I used to think that top environmental problems were biodiversity loss, ecosystem collapse and climate change. I thought that thirty years of good science could address these problems. I was wrong. The top environmental problems are selfishness, greed and apathy, and to deal with these we need a cultural and spiritual transformation. And we scientists don't know how to do that."[53] Samulel Ebimgbo and others from the University of Nigeria write that even atheists and agnostics have some form of belief that they hold on to.[54] As such, it is not uncommon in social work practice also for clients to express or refer to their spirituality in one way or another.

As a matter of fact, the spiritual makeup of any person is as important as her or his biological, psychological and social makeup.[55] Therefore, it

---

48. Niekerk, "Spirituality and Religion," 9.
49. Vilani et al., "Role of Spirituality," 6.
50. ASA, "Religion and Spirituality."
51. Tirkey, *Outline of Spirituality*, 11.
52. Ebimgbo et al., *Spirituality and Religion*, 93.
53. Speth, "Living on Earth."
54. Ebimgbo et al., *Spirituality and Religion*, 93.
55. Manfred-Gilham, "Experiential Approach"; Loue, *Social Work Values*.

would not be comprehensive to talk about social work ethics without taking into consideration the role of spirituality in social work.

In an article on "The Place of Spirituality in Social Work: Practitioners' Personal Views and Beliefs", Garcia-Irons clearly states and convincingly demonstrates that the origins of social work are founded in the practices of spirituality and religion.[56] The just cited author further writes that in the mid-1800s, establishments called charitable organizations in England were made up of church personnel and volunteers who were designated to help the poor, homeless, and severely ill people in society. Accordingly, the principles underlying those early social work practices were founded on the biblical idea of charity, which is very similar to the historical development of common law as discussed in the previous section. Therefore, the concept of spirituality in social work has definite implications for the ethical evaluation of philanthropic strategies implemented by charitable organizations.

Due to the secularization of social work, especially in the 1960s and 1970s, spirituality and religion kind of separated themselves from the field, so that they eventually have become a topic that is little talked about in social work.[57] Recent research, however, shows the there is a renewed call for the integration of spirituality into social work practice and education.[58] As at the time of conducting research for the thesis on which this book is based, the then just ended European Symposium on Spirituality, Ethics and Social Work identified spirituality both as an approach to and a phenomenon within social work practice and education.[59]

It is, however, still difficult to immediately standardize the definition of spirituality in social work because of its complexity and recent focal inclusion into social work practice and education, which is also a modern secular profession.[60] In spite of this fact and for the sake of better understanding, it is still possible and prudent to refer to some of the significant and more comprehensive definitions so far.

Among others, Verna Carson, a retired professor, clinical nurse specialist in psychiatric mental health nursing, and consultant at Towson University, is cited saying:

---

56. Garcia-Irons, *Place of Spirituality*, 1–7.
57. Popple and Leighninger, *Social Work, Social Welfare*, 186–99.
58. Ebimgbo et al., *Spirituality and Religion*; Garcia-Irons, *Place of Spirituality*, 1.
59. Gehrig et al., "Spirituality in Social Work."
60. Gray, "Viewing Spirituality," 176–80; Holden, *Jehovah's Witnesses*, 37.

## LITERATURE SURVEY

> To be spiritual is to stand in a relationship to another based on matters of the soul. Spirituality is the way we make meaning out of our lives. It is the recognition of the presence of Spirit within us and a cultivation of a style of life consistent with that presence. Spirituality provides a perspective to foster purpose, meaning and direction to live. It may find expression through religion.[61]

Edward Canda and Leola Furman define spirituality as "a universal quality of human beings and their cultures related to the quest for meaning, purpose, morality, transcendence, well-being, and profound relationships with ourselves and others, leading to an ultimate reality."[62] Harold Koenig and David Larson also observe that spirituality "is the personal quest for understanding answers to ultimate questions about life, about meaning, and about relationship to the sacred or transcendent, which may (or may not) lead to or arise from the development of religious rituals and formation of community."[63]

Joyce Rumun Akpenpuun, senior lecturer of medical sociology at Benue State University in Nigeria, states that spirituality entails a deeper dimension to human life and an inner world of the soul, while Patrick Nmah of Enugu State University perceives spirituality as incorporating faith in order to advance given objectives such as a high state of awareness, out of reach of wisdom, or communion with God or creation.[64] He further writes that spirituality includes introspection and the development of an individual's inner life through practices such as meditation, prayer and contemplation.

With regard to the topic under exploration in this book, social work involves dealing with a complex relationship between professional and spiritual values.[65] As such, it is inevitable to approach the aspect of social work ethics from a spiritual point of view as well. Edna Lezotte writes that religious and spiritual beliefs and practices are part of our multicultural diversity.[66] Therefore, social workers should also have knowledge and skills in the area of spirituality in order to be able to work effectively with diverse

---

61. Cf. Lezotte, "Spirituality and Social Work," 2.
62. Canda and Furman, *Spiritual Diversity in Social Work*, 5.
63. Koenig and Larson, "Religion and Mental Health," 1.
64. See Akpenpuun, "Influence of Religious Beliefs," 27–48; Nmah, "Christian Fundamentalism in Nigeria," 321–37.
65. Neagoe, "Ethical Dilemmas of the Social Work," 1.
66. Lezotte, "Spirituality and Social Work," 7.

categories of clients. The just cited author explicitly states that there is another dimension of human existence beyond the bio-psychosocial framework that can be used to understand human behavior, and social work education should expand its framework to include the spiritual dimension of human existence as well.

Apparently, an overwhelming amount of literature reveals that a majority of social workers feel that they do not have the appropriate training to utilize spirituality in their practice, while others even express ambivalence and anxiety around spirituality.[67] Mel Gray, a powerful advocate for social work that is both theoretically informed and evidence based, also writes that authors in the field of spirituality lament the lack of training for social workers to deal with spiritual issues, especially of the clients.[68] According to Alexis Garcia-Irons, the discrepancy between the desire for more common use of spirituality in social work practice in the field and the lack of formal training and education on the topic has ethical implications for the philanthropic social work field too.[69]

For example, by being incompetent in the spiritual dimension, social workers may be depriving clients of an opportunity to explore a topic or source of strength and hope that may otherwise help them. For instance, spirituality has been presented to be a major positive coping factor through therapy when helping those living with HIV/AIDS or dealing with sexual self-esteem.[70] Michael Sheridan and others also observe that sometimes a client may have a very strong connection to her or his faith or spiritual practice, but hardly finds a social worker who is sufficiently prepared to speak on the topic and figure out how it fits in helping the respective client.[71]

With regard to the subject hereby under investigation, the obvious ethical question that arises is whether the charitable organizations operating among African communities have the appropriate training and education to deal with issues of African spiritualities in the execution of their philanthropic strategies, especially in a country like Zambia that is a self-confessed Christian nation?

67. Belcher and Mellinger, "Integrating Spirituality," 377–94; Bullis, *Spirituality in Social Work*; Carrington, "Integrated Spiritual Practice," 287–312; Moss, "Spirituality and Social Care," 578–80; Oxhandler and Parrish, "Integrating Clients' Religion/Spirituality," 680–94.
68. Gray, "Viewing Spirituality," 176–77.
69. Garcia-Irons, *Place of Spirituality*, 2.
70. Seinfeld, "Spirituality in Social Work," 240–44.
71. Sheridan et al., "Practitioners," 190–203.

## Literature Survey

### *Ethical Dilemmas and Ethical Decision-Making in Social Work*

Ethical dilemmas are conflicts that arise when two or more ethical principles clash.[72] The just previous section connects directly with the question of ethical dilemmas in social work as it involves dealing with a complex relationship between professional and spiritual values. For example, should a social worker bend the rules for allocating home care services to help a very needy person, or follow a criteria and refuse the application? In this case the social worker is faced with a conflict between principle and duty in following rules and criteria that apply to everyone. Such ethical dilemmas as this are not uncommon in the practice of philanthropic social work. Erik Blennberger and Titti Fränkel provide a list of common ethical dilemmas in social work, though without claim for exhaustiveness, as follows:

i. Care, support and assistance versus control and demands.

ii. The risk of a seemingly necessary caring attitude leading to the loss of a person's own power of initiative and sense of dignity.

iii. Respect for a person's right to self-determination and freedoms versus the risk of one's efforts leading to the stigmatization of that person and their wounded self-esteem.

iv. Difficulties in treating clients with respect and of creating a positive relationship in a job that has unavoidable elements of demand and control.

v. Maintaining democratic values such as individual freedoms and equal opportunities for both sexes versus showing admiration for persons and groups who do not uphold these values.

vi. The conflict between, on the one hand, defending or protecting certain clients and, on the other, taking into consideration the interests of those closely related and others.

vii. The right of the child to advantageous living conditions versus the right of the parents to exert their parentage and live their family lives on their own terms.

viii. Prioritizing time and resources between different client categories with different needs.

---

72. Malinga et al., "Ethical Dilemmas."

ix. Carrying out measures deemed necessary and proper versus demands for economic stringency.

x. Maintaining loyalty with the work and the organization, even when one finds policy and working conditions to be contrary to well-founded practice and the best interests of the client, and perhaps also to juridical norms for the work.

xi. Conflicts of loyalty between defending the client's best interests and support and defense of a colleague.[73]

How social workers resolve ethical dilemmas has been a subject of rising concern. With focus on ethical dilemmas, Sarah Banks writes that textbooks on social work ethics often include significant sections on decision-making about how to act in difficult situations.[74] According to Elaine Congress, professor and associate dean for special programs at Fordham University, social workers in this regard should be guided by two main principles, namely beneficence (positive obligation), which speaks of providing good, and non-malfeasance (negative obligation), which relate to causing no harm.[75] Accordingly, social workers who prefer beneficence are most likely to take a proactive stance, while those who favor non-malfeasance are likely to opt for the least intervention such as taking no action and waiting for further results. Ultimately, however, both principles affect ethical decision-making.

Furthermore, whether knowingly or unknowingly, social workers usually appeal to two philosophical models—deontological and teleological—in resolving ethical dilemmas as Elaine Congress rightly observes.[76] The just cited authority and Frederic Reamer also write that deontological thinkers believe that social work values such as confidentiality and self-determination are so absolute and definitive of the profession that to deny them would lead to distrust or disrepute of the profession.[77] Many social workers, however, use a teleological approach, which involves examining the consequences of a situation or decision.[78] Congress further writes that

---

73. Blennberger and Fränkel, *Ethics in Social Work*.

74. Banks, "Social Work Ethics," 11–12. See, e.g., Bowles et al., *Ethical Practice in Social Work*; Dolgoff et al., *Ethical Decisions in Social Work*; Reamer, *Social Work Values*.

75. Congress, "What Social Workers Should Know," 9.

76. Congress, "What Social Workers Should Know," 9.

77. Reamer, "Ethical Theories," 17–19.

78. Congress, "What Social Workers Should Know," 9.

most social workers actually employ a combination of deontological and teleological thinking in resolving ethical dilemmas.

As such, one would rationalize that although values of social work profession are deontological in nature, social workers usually use teleological consequential arguments to decide complex ethical dilemmas.[79] Both Congress and Reamer further observe that most social workers, actually, do not use a philosophical approach at all but base their decisions on other models of practical wisdom and moral reasoning when faced with ethical dilemmas, which is akin to practical moral reasoning discussed under ethical perspectives from practical theology.[80] Sarah Banks cites Elaine Congress's five-step ETHIC model as one of the most cited linear approaches to deciding on ethical dilemmas as hereafter presented.

- E  Examine personal, cultural, societal, client, agency and professional values.
- T  Think about the various UN declarations on rights and related covenants, codes of ethics, laws and agency regulations.
- H  Hypothesize different courses of action based on varied decisions.
- I  Identify who is most vulnerable, who will be harmed or helped.
- C  Consult with supervisors and colleagues.[81]

This is a simple and user-friendly model that can help social workers to make ethical decisions in circumstances when they are faced with ethical dilemmas.

*Summary of Ethical Perspectives from Social Work*

Principles of social justice, human rights, collective responsibility and respect for diversities underpin social work practice. Apparently, the discourse of social work is also enriched significantly by theological ethics through the latter's emphatic criticism of the limited focus of professional ethics of social work, which focus mainly on deontological and utilitarian ethics.

---

79. Congress, "What Social Workers Should Know," 10.
80. Reamer, "Ethical Theories," 20.
81. Banks, "Social Work Ethics," 12. See also Congress, *Social Work Values*.

Although the issue of ethics in social work is not easy to reconcile globally, which is customary of social work discourse, it is generally accepted that ethics in social work can be summed up into six fundamental foci, namely: social justice, service, dignity and worth of the human person, integrity, importance of human relationships, and competence. These ethical categories or perspectives are directly applicable to the evaluation of ethics in philanthropy under study in this book.

Another area of ethical consideration from the perspective of social work concerns spirituality in social work since the origins of social work have been located in the practices of spirituality and religion and the principles thereof are based on the biblical idea of charity. The discrepancy between the rising concerns for more common use of spirituality in social work practice in the field and the lack of formal training and education on the topic poses serious ethical implications for the field of social work. As such, the perspective of spirituality in social work has definite implications for the subject under investigation.

Ethical dilemmas arise when two or more ethical principles clash and this calls for ethical decision-making or practical moral reasoning.

Next are ethical perspectives from common law with regard to ethics in philanthropy.

## Ethical Perspectives from Common Law

From the perspective of common law, the ethical evaluation of philanthropic strategies of charitable organizations operating among African communities will be based on a threefold criterion of theoretical interpretation, ethical reflection, and good practice.[82]

### *Theoretical Interpretation of Charitable Organizations and Purposes*

Theoretical interpretation is the ability to draw on theories of the arts and sciences in order to understand and respond to particular episodes, situations, and contexts.[83] It is important to highlight from the outset that correct theoretical interpretation is as critical in this study as in any other because correct interpretation produces correct results while wrong

82. Osmer, *Practical Theology*, 161.
83. Osmer, *Practical Theology*, 83.

interpretation produces wrong results.[84] As such, it is important to have correct theoretical interpretation of charitable organizations and purposes in order to come up with a correct ethical evaluation of philanthropic strategies of charitable organizations.

The original Greek concept of "theory" (*theōria*) in itself neither meant science nor connoted a scientific construct or model. According to Austin Harrington's classical book on modern social theory published by Oxford University Press, *"theōria"* rather implied a reflection on science and its values as one mode of contemplating the cosmos, including art, myth, religion, and the most general discipline of thinking that the Greeks called "philosophy", which basically means "love of wisdom."[85] This is in tandem with Hannah Arendt's long-held view of a world where theory and philosophy do not only assist but also remind science of its ethical obligations amidst the fragility of the earth's resources and mortality of the human life.[86]

Therefore, it follows that theoretical interpretation of charity and charitable purposes should remind charities of their ethical obligations as they design their respective philanthropic strategies. Despite the fact that there is no common definition for charity and philanthropy, common law latitude still dictates that there is enough societal jurisprudence to guide philanthropic strategies of charitable organizations towards moral ends. Jakobus Vorster,[87] a senior researcher at North-West University, maintains that there is a sense of justice that is written and stamped on every person's heart and mind, respectively, and the civil authority has the obligation to develop this law and thus administer justice properly. As Jan van Wyk and Nicolaas Vorster[88] also rightly observe, even constitutions and laws are written from particular perspectives that are determined by worldviews.

In his award winning book on foreign policy, *The Bottom Billion: Why the Poorest Countries Are Failing and What Can Be Done About It*, Paul Collier, a former head of research at the World Bank, writes that most conduct is guided by societal norms rather than laws.[89] According to Collier, the world has so far generated a huge range of norms that are even enshrined

---

84. Vorster, *Ethical Perspectives on Human Rights*, 19.
85. Harrington, *Modern Social Theory*, 2.
86. See Arendt, *Human Condition*.
87. Vorster, *Ethical Perspectives on Human Rights*, 30–31.
88. Wyk and Vorster, "Introduction," 9.
89. Collier, *Bottom Billion*, 139.

in international standards and codes of conduct. He further postulates that most of these norms are voluntary, but some of them ultimately carry the force of the law and can be massively effective even in inducing changes in governance. Such is common law with regard to charities and philanthropy, which in this case enforces that a charity must have a charitable purpose and be for the benefit of the public.[90]

The ethical question arising from the foregoing theoretical interpretation is whether the philanthropic strategies of charitable organizations that operate among African communities adhere to the dictates of common law pertaining to charities and charitable purposes? This question leads to the next aspect of ethical reflection from the perspective of common law.

*Ethical Reflection on Charitable Organizations and Purposes*

Ethical reflection is the use of ethical principles, rules, or guidelines to direct action toward moral ends.[91] In this case, it comes close to developing normative perspective on boundary issues that cannot be crossed by our discourse of philanthropic strategies of charitable organizations. Mel Thompson, in his book *Understanding Ethics*, writes that "when thinking about any problem it is important to start by establishing own foundational values, namely principles that you are unwilling to compromise."[92] Suffice it to state that this is not a matter of importing ethics into the problematic situation, but rather the recognition that such norms and values already are a part of a problem solving process or research.[93] According to Don S. Browning, the application of such norms does not only occur at the end of a study, but is present from the beginning and influences it right through.[94]

The ethical aspects hereafter discussed emanate from a critical reflection of the contextual and core issues presented in chapter 1, as well as from some sections of this chapter such as the historical development of charity law and social work perspectives. They include equality and fairness, right to self-determination, deserving and undeserving poor, transparency and accountability, as well as good practice.

---

90. Martin, "Legal Concept of Charity," 20.
91. Osmer, *Practical Theology*, 161.
92. Thompson, *Understanding Ethics*, 107.
93. Osmer, *Practical Theology*, 149.
94. Browning, *Fundamental Practical Theology*, 39.

LITERATURE SURVEY

## Equality and Fairness

The aspects of equality and fairness in this context emanate from the issue that triggered the research for this book and, specifically, with regard to ethical guidelines for responsible giving as outlined by Ted Lechterman, such as giving to the neediest, giving mindfully, giving to heal and address injustices, and to overcome unjust policies.[95] In the charitable purposes as expanded by the Charities Act of 2006 for England and Wales, these are directly implicit in such charitable purposes as the advancement of human rights, conflict resolution or reconciliation, promotion of religious or racial harmony, equality, and diversity as well as the relief of those in need by reason of youth, age, ill health, disability, financial hardship, or other disabilities.[96] Elsewhere, equality and fairness are also directly implicit in ethical perspectives from social work such as social justice as well as dignity and worth of the human person.

Equality and fairness are as cardinal to the philanthropic strategies of charitable organizations as elsewhere in order for real socio-economic transformation to take place in the communities among which these organizations operate. This is so because all humans are worthy of respect in personal relationships and fair treatment in social institutions and before the law.[97] Suffice to recapitulate that it is the quest for equality and fairness that undergirded the court's decision in the historic Pemsel's Case of 1891: as hereafter cited:

> If I could accept, without reserve, the opinions expressed in Baird's Trustees with respect to the meaning of the term "charitable," I should still entertain doubts as to the rule applied to its decision, which has been followed in this case by the majority of the English judges. The only principle derivable from Lord Saltoun v. Lord Advocate, which can aid in the decision of this case, appears to me to be this—that the Act of 1842 must, if possible, be so interpreted as to make the incidence of its taxation the same in both countries. In that case the language which the Court had to construe, which was not technical, had, when read in the light of the context, the effect of producing the equality which the legislature presumably contemplated.[98]

95. Lechterman, "Ethical Guide to Responsible Giving."
96. Proirier, *Charity Law in New Zealand*, 87.
97. Osmer, *Practical Theology*, 51.
98. Halsbury et al., *Commissioners v. Pemsel*, 15.

In the discourse of his work on *Understanding Political Philosophy*, Mel Thompson stresses that equality and fairness are foundational values for economic transformation and growth.[99] In his corresponding work, *Understanding Ethics*, Thompson further discusses that whereas success is perceived to be more of an economic feature, the question of whether economic growth should be the only consideration for success is an ethical question.[100] As stated in the first chapter, it is not ethically acceptable that the end always justifies the means because actions and processes that lead to a desirable end ought to be as desirable and acceptable as the desired end.

In the case of this particular study, it is expected of the charitable organizations that operate among poor African communities to design and implement philanthropic strategies that enhance equality and fairness of the people, especially in aspects such as distribution of resources, respect in relationships, and fair treatment in social and legal institutions.

## Right to Self-Determination

The contextual issues presented in chapter 1 have also revealed that indigenous peoples in different parts of the world have experienced rapid culture change, marginalization, and absorption into a global economy with negligible regard for their autonomy, a threat that borders on a people's right to self-determination. According to the Unrepresented Nations and Peoples Organisation (UNPO), the right to self-determination is essentially "the right of a people to determine its own destiny. In particular, the principle allows a people to choose its own political status and to determine its own form of economic, cultural and social development."[101]

A critical issue with philanthropic strategies employed by charitable organizations, which in this case are international NGOs and FBOs in Africa, is whether the changes and absorptions into global economic systems brought about by their strategies take care of the indigenous people's autonomous identities or rather marginalize the poor and vulnerable people. Laurence Kirmayer and others observe that indigenous people are usually absorbed into a global economy with little or no regard for their autonomous identities, which should not be the case.[102]

---

99. Thompson, *Understanding Political Philosophy*, 107–10.

100. Thompson, *Understanding Ethics*, 129.

101. UNPO, "Self-Determination."

102. Kirmayer et al., *Mental Health of Indigenous Peoples*, 5.

## Literature Survey

I can cite a related practical example from one of my previous studies that involved a local community and an external FBO that funded the project through the local church.[103] According to the funding organization, the perceived need was forest preservation, but that was an inaccurate perception. It became evident from my interviews with the local people that the real pressing need was their human survival. The desperate state of poverty in which the local people found themselves was a strong determinant of other human and environmental problems, a perspective that is also supported by Hennie Swanepoel and Erik de Beer's work on breaking the cycle of poverty in community development.[104] The people were cutting down trees, not with the ill-intention to destroy the environment, but as a desperate survival means. That was the real issue at hand, but the international charity mistakenly funded something else.

Learning from this example and several others, it is imperative for local communities to fully participate in both the formulation and implementation of philanthropic strategies intended for them, rather than merely trying out foreign concepts without due adherence to the autonomous identity and dynamics of their local context. As it were, a key feature of economic transformation is action at grassroots, where the affected people themselves take the leading part, with external experts and NGOs playing a facilitating role.[105] As Paul Collier writes, "Change in the societies at the very bottom must come predominantly from within."[106] This means that the initiative, drive, and ownership of the change process must come predominately from within the affected community members themselves. Collier, nevertheless, also acknowledges that there is still need for external technical and physical resources such as charitable organizations, foreign aid, and international policies, but to assist and strengthen local initiatives.[107]

Suffice it to mention that one of the common dangers with some philanthropic strategies such as welfare approaches is that they can actually disempower local people and cause dependency as Rachel Blackman also rightly observes.[108] Accordingly, outside resources have only second order effect on poverty alleviation and community transformation, which is to

---

103. Mutemwa, "Effectiveness of Sesheke Church," 163.
104. Swanepoel and Beer, *Community Development*, 111.
105. Swanepoel and Beer, *Community Development*, 44.
106. Collier, *Bottom Billion*, 9, 71.
107. Collier, *Bottom Billion*, 99–123.
108. Blackman, *Partnering with the Local Church*, 30–32.

strengthen inside initiatives. The first order effect must come from within the affected people themselves. As such, the focus of philanthropic strategies by charitable organizations should be on increasing self-reliance of the local people such as through income generation initiatives as Blackman further writes.[109] In this regard, the charitable organizations are expected, with the cooperation of local structures, to help individuals and communities attain sustainable transformational development through technical, physical, and financial support that enhance bigger and long term transformational initiatives.[110] Therefore, the local communities must pay attention to the incentives and philanthropic strategies that enable local households to adjust their production systems and livelihoods in ways that guarantee both welfare and sustainable economic growth.[111] This would ensure sustainable development strategies without compromising the local people's right to self-determination.

## Deserving and Undeserving Poor

The issue of the deserving and undeserving poor is also tied to the observation made in the first chapter that donors should reflect more on their giving decisions and, among others, give to the neediest, not necessarily the nearest. In common law, this is directly implicit in the historical development of charity law, where the English state under Queen Elizabeth I had to distinguish between the poor who merited help and those who did not because they could work and help themselves. Said another way, not all those who were poor deserved help because others among them could work and help themselves.

The question of who deserves and who does not deserve help has a very long history—from about the late eighteenth century, according to Michael Katz—and has particular implications too for the topic and scope of this book.[112] Apart from other reasons such as policy issues, the impulse to categorically classify the deserving and undeserving poor has persisted for centuries because resources are also limited in the sense that neither the state nor private charities can distribute them in unlimited quantities to

---

109. Blackman, *Partnering with the Local Church*, 30.
110. Hoek and Yardley, *Keeping Communities Clean*, 6.
111. Pender et al., "Strategies for Sustainable Development," 1.
112. Katz, *Undeserving Poor*, 1.

# Literature Survey

all who might claim need. Katz provides valid guidance towards a possible solution in form of three questions as follows:

i. How can we draw boundaries between who does and who does not merit help?

ii. How can we provide help without increasing dependency or creating moral hazard?

iii. What are the limits of social responsibility (what do we owe to the poor and to each other)?

Such questions as the foregoing do form an integral part of a theoretical base or framework that can be used to ethically evaluate the philanthropic strategies employed charitable organizations operating among poor African communities such as Mongu district in the Western province of Zambia.

The quest to distinguish between the deserving and undeserving poor is also implicit in the factors that preceded and precipitated the Elizabeth Statute of Charitable Uses of 1601. Fiona Martin records that as poverty increased and became a matter of national concern in England, the English state under Elizabeth I intervened and established workhouses to discipline and make productive the poor who could work and also required of local parishes to provide for their own poor.[113] The state later turned to encourage private philanthropy due to its own bankruptcy to assist the other category of poor people who were genuinely impotent of work. What is clear here is that the state's first approach was to distinguish between the deserving and undeserving poor. The philosophical thought underpinning this concept is that poverty is not only the result of being in need, but also of failings and fecklessness among the poor as Pete Dorey observes.[114] As such, there is need to include criteria for critically distinguishing between the deserving and undeserving poor in the evaluation of philanthropic strategies that are being employed by charitable organizations such as operate in Africa.

The principle on which the laws of the poor rested divided the poor into two categories, namely the "impotent poor" (deserving) and the "able poor" (undeserving poor) as Michael Katz records.[115] Accordingly, the impotent poor were those wholly incapable of work due to genuine reasons

---

113. Martin, "Legal Concept of Charity," 21.
114. Dorey, *Sage Encyclopedia of World Poverty*, 1.
115. Katz, *Undeserving Poor*, 5.

such as old age, infancy, sickness, or corporeal debility. The able poor, on the other hand, were those who were capable of some work of one nature or another, but deferring in the degree of their capacity and in the kind of work of which they were capable.

The question of whether help is deserved or not is still as important for now as before because it entails not only an evaluation of the scale of financial hardships or poverty, but also an ethical judgment concerning the degree of culpability.[116] This is a useful basic criterion for distinguishing between the deserving and undeserving poor that can be employed in an ethical evaluation of philanthropic strategies implemented by charitable organizations operating among poor African communities.

### Transparency and Accountability

The issue that triggered the research for this book is the fact that next to nothing was known about the ethical obligations and operational strategies of most charitable organizations in Mongu district and Zambia as a country as revealed in the contexts that called for the investigation presented in chapter 1. This issue seriously borders on lack of transparency and accountability. Furthermore, it has been argued in the wider context of literature research even outside Zambia that in some cases the information provided by charitable organizations could be inadequate or misleading for effective monitoring and regulation of the charities such as was the case in Malaysia.[117] In the historical development of charity law, a major aim of the enactment of the Statute of Charitable Uses 1601 was to provide checks and balances, that is, transparency and accountability, to the administration of most charities and to prevent any misuse of charitable property as Fiona Martin records.[118]

Since then, the aspect of transparency and accountability has become an increasingly serious ethical issue with regard to the operations of charitable organizations as donors begun to signal that they were not happy with the level of information provided so far by the charities they funded.[119] The Statute of Charitable Uses 1601 also aimed at appointing a bishop of a local diocese and the gentry as commissioners to supervise

---

116. Dorey, *Sage Encyclopedia of World Poverty*, 1.
117. Hasnan et al., *Issues, Challenges*, 777.
118. Martin, "Legal Concept of Charity," 21.
119. Iwaarden et al., "Charities," 5.

the administration of most charities. This was to ensure transparency and accountability. According to Suhaily Hasnan and others, in many cases the information reported by the charitable organizations is either insufficient or misrepresentative for effective monitoring and regulation of the charities involved.[120] In similar vein, Ruhaya Atan and others also observe that there is information asymmetry and a lack of transparency between non-profit organizations (NPOs) and donors and that the NPOs, especially charities, need to improve on their transparency and accountability.[121]

The foregoing discourse directly applies to International NGOs and FBOs that operate among poor African communities as explained earlier in chapter 1 that next to nothing was known about their operations among the local communities in Zambia, not even by the oversight government departments.[122] This scenario poses enough danger to warrant an urgent ethical evaluation of the philanthropic strategies employed by charitable organizations that operate among poor and naïve African communities. To buttress it, substantial amounts of literature and empirical research have revealed that there is a causative relationship between the extent of disclosure levels and the amount of future donations received.[123] That is to say, the amount of future donations to be received either increases or decreases with the extent to which the disclosure level increases or decreases, respectively. For example, Van Iwaarden and others observe that at least two thirds of Americans are losing trust in charities because they did not know how the charities were spending their money.[124] Therefore, if not ethically checked, even well-meaning charitable organizations operating among poor African communities might lose their trustworthiness from funders and, consequently, fail to yield desirable results due to diminishing or stopped funding.

In view of the foregoing, there is dire need to develop criteria to enhance transparency and accountability of charitable organizations that operate in Africa for both public benefit and donor trust. According to Iwaarden et al., measurement of a charity's performance is a complex matter that is easier said than done.[125] The co-authors, however, consider

120. Hasnan et al., *Issues, Challenges*, 777.
121. Atan et al., *Quality Information*, 118.
122. MCDSS, *NGO File 2018*, 1, 7–9.
123. Atan et al., *Quality Information*, 119.
124. Iwaarden et al., "Charities," 6.
125. Iwaarden et al., "Charities," 7.

measurements of internal efficiency and external effectiveness to be effective in addressing the complexities associated with measuring performances of charities. With regard to internal efficiency, as Woods Bowman reckons, most donors expect worthy charitable organizations to have lower administrative and fundraising costs than project expenditure costs.[126] According to both Bowman and Iwaarden et al., it is commonly accepted that program expenditure should be not less than 65 percent of the total expenditure, while the administrative and fundraising costs should be at most 35 percent.

With regard to external effectiveness, it is preferable to measure what is possible rather than what is important—a tendency which manifests in measuring specific projects or programs instead of the whole organization.[127] Although the relationship between the effectiveness of individual charitable programs and the overall effectiveness of a charitable organizations is still being studied, Iwaarden and others still note that it is much easier to assess the effectiveness of a particular program than a whole organization.[128]

By implication, measurements of internal efficiency and external effectiveness would be helpful in enhancing the levels of transparency and accountability with regard to philanthropic strategies of charitable organizations that operate in developing or underdeveloped parts of the world, particularly in Africa.

## Good Practice

Good practice involves deriving acceptable norms from exploring models of such practice in the present and past, or by engaging reflexivity in transforming practice in the present.[129] As such, the historical development of common law concerning charities and charitable purposes discussed earlier in this chapter is in itself also an aspect of good practice. The ethical reflection on universal ethical principles in the background context and guidelines for responsible giving as outlined by Ted Lechterman (as cited in

---

126. Bowman, "Should Donors Care," 288–310.

127. Cunningham and Ricks, "Why Measure?," 44–51; Iwaarden et al., "Charities," 8–9.

128. Iwaarden et al., "Charities," 9.

129. Osmer, *Practical Theology*, 161.

chapter 1) also entail good practice with regard to the scope of this book.[130] A summative recapitulation of the respective guidelines is hereby provided: giving from the heart, giving to the neediest, giving mindfully, giving to heal and address injustices, giving to overcome unjust policies, and mixing and matching.

In the broader perspective, other models of good practice can be derived from charitable organizations such as the Charity Organization Society (COS) formed in England in 1869 for the purpose of providing a much greater degree of coherence and coordination to the hundreds of disparate and ad hoc voluntary bodies and philanthropic groups that dealt with the poor during the latter half of the nineteenth century.[131] The COS did not, however, involve itself in providing direct support financially or in kind, but rather sought to liaise with other charities by referring "deserving cases" to them while encouraging such voluntary bodies to adhere to a set of shared principles. So the role of the COS was to promote and disseminate good practice with regard to philanthropic activities by charitable organizations. Such a model as this can also be very helpful towards evaluating the ethical aspects of philanthropic strategies by charitable organizations that operate among poor African communities.

Finally, suffice it to deduce that the aspects of theoretical interpretation and ethical reflection explored in this section also constitute good practice with regard to the subject hereby under study. For better understanding, this can be presented in form of a linear equation as follows:

Theoretical Interpretation + Ethical Reflection = Good Practice.

## Summary of Ethical Perspectives from Common Law

The ethical perspectives from common law with regard to philanthropic strategies of charitable organizations such as operate in Africa have been based on a threefold criterion of theoretical interpretation, ethical reflection, and good practice. Accordingly, theoretical interpretation of charity and charitable purposes should remind charities of their ethical obligations as they design their respective philanthropic strategies. Similarly, common law enforces that a charity must have a charitable purpose and be for the benefit of the public. The ethical question arising from theoretical interpretation of charity and charitable purpose is whether the philanthropic

---

130. Lechterman, "Ethical Guide to Responsible Giving."
131. Dorey, *Sage Encyclopedia of World Poverty*, 1–3.

strategies of charitable organizations operating in Africa adhere to the dictates of common law pertaining to charities and charitable purposes?

Ethical reflection included aspects of equality and fairness, right to self-determination, deserving and undeserving poor, and transparency and accountability. Good practice also applies directly to the aspect of common law concerning charities and charitable purposes as it involves deriving acceptable norms from exploring models of such practice in the present and past or by engaging reflexivity in transforming practice in the present. Suffice it to infer that the aspects of theoretical interpretation and ethical reflection also constitute good practice with regard to the subject under exploration in this book.

## SUMMARY OF PERSPECTIVES FROM LITERATURE SURVEY

Understanding the historical development of charity law is necessary for its correct application. The current definition of charity and charitable purpose is based on over four hundred years of common law since the Statute of Charitable Uses 1601. Therefore, it is important to understand the historical background of this law because it is the evolution of charity law around the Statute of Charitable Uses 1601 that still resonates in law to date. As such, it forms an important framework for the topic of this book too.

Finally, this chapter has located the theoretical framework for the ethical evaluation of philanthropic strategies by charitable organizations within an interdisciplinary perspective of theological and sociological discourses comprising pastoral theology, social work, and common law.

Next is the approach.

# 4

# The Approach

## INTRODUCTION

Initially, my approach to the issue at hand as explained in the previous chapter was to advocate for policy formulation to govern charitable organizations in the country, so as to effectively address the issue of ethicality of philanthropic strategies employed by charitable organizations operating in local communities. As it were, without a governing policy at national level, it was not possible to correct the problematic situation at local level. However, as per the comprehension of the complexity and magnitude of the issue, it became apparent that there were both local and global influences at play in the local situation. The demand for ethicality of philanthropic strategies in this case weighs more on the provider than recipient of charitable aid. As such, it was necessary to come up with an approach that would help to address the ethicality of charitable organizations locally and globally, especially that most of the charitable organizations operating among poor African communities are from the more developed Western countries.

Based on the background contextual and core issues, the overarching question that arises is how to evaluate the ethical aspects of philanthropic strategies employed by charitable organizations operating among poor African communities such as Mongu district of Western Zambia? In order to address this question satisfactorily, related cognitive theoretical, empirical, and pragmatic issues ought to be addressed. For instance, what kind of theoretical perspectives could enrich our understanding of the ethical aspects of philanthropic strategies employed by charitable organizations operating among poor African communities? Which perspectives could be descriptive-empirical evidence of the ethical aspects of philanthropic strategies employed by these charitable organizations? And, what kind of critical pragmatic reflection would constitute an ideal model for the ethical evaluation of philanthropic strategies employed by charitable organizations?

As it were, the aim of writing this book is to present a model for evaluating ethical aspects of philanthropic strategies employed by charitable organizations operating among poor African communities. To develop a robust and consistent argument, specific objectives related to the theoretical, empirical, and pragmatic perspectives of the issue at hand should be achieved.

Accordingly, in my study I had to operationalize the charitable organizations operating in Africa and related concepts in order to come up with an appropriate ethical evaluation of philanthropic strategies employed by the said charities. In like manner, I had to determine, through literature review in the broader spectrum, theoretical perspectives that could enrich our understanding of ethical aspects of philanthropic strategies employed by charitable organizations that operated among poor African communities.

Second, I took time to conduct a systematic empirical case study research to discover perspectives that could be descriptive-empirical evidence of the ethical aspects of philanthropic strategies employed by charitable organizations that operated among poor African countries such as Mongu district. The results and discussions of my empirical investigations are presented later in the next chapter.

My third task was to develop, through critical pragmatic reflection on the findings of the preceding objectives, a model to guide the ethical evaluation of philanthropic strategies employed by charitable organizations. As it were, real science requires that there should be some rational connection between explanatory theory and empirical evidence.[1]

## CENTRAL THEORETICAL THOUGHT AND SIGNIFICANCE

My central theoretical thought underpinning the text of this book is that an ethical evaluation of philanthropic strategies employed by charitable organizations will enlighten the government, educators, NGOs, local communities, and wider society of the ethical aspects at stake in the implementation of philanthropic strategies by various NGOs. In turn, this will enhance

---

1. Murphy, *Reasoning and Rhetoric*, 13.

THE APPROACH

ethicality and professionalism of the charitable organizations and optimize benefits to the local communities through ethically acceptable means.

I am, therefore, under the impression that this book will contribute significantly to the understanding of philanthropic social work with regard to ethics in charity from an indigenous African context and perspective, while taking into consideration the global influences and concepts at play in the local situation. As it were, even if research findings are valid within their specific time, space, and value context, it is also a proven fact and principle that understanding the meaning of a phenomenon in its context enhances understanding of phenomena in other similar situations because system are nestled within other systems in the web of life.[2]

## STRATEGY OF INQUIRY

For better understanding and adherence to academic rigor and criticism, I am compelled to present in brevity the strategy of inquiry I followed to ensure credibility of the information contained in this book. As it were, there are basically two strategies of inquiry in research, namely, qualitative and quantitative research, although some researchers have come up with a mixed methods approach.[3] What determines a strategy of inquiry to be used in a given research, however, is the nature of the problem being addressed and general purpose of the inquiry.[4]

As such, the strategy of inquiry that I employed for the case study was qualitative research because it tends to work better with relatively small numbers or cases and finds detail in the precise particulars of such matters as the people's understandings and interactions.[5] Quantitative research, on the other hand, could not adequately address the nature of the problem and guiding purpose of the study because it was not the goal of my study to gather and analyze numeric data in order to explore relationships among variables as embraced by quantitative research.[6] Rather, the study aimed at evaluating ethical aspects of philanthropic strategies employed by a specific

---

2. Botes, "Functional Approach," 22; Burns and Grove, *Practice of Nursing Research*, 29; Osmer, *Practical Theology*, 200.

3. Creswell, *Research Design* [2003]; Osmer, *Practical Theology*, 49.

4. Creswell, *Research Design* [2014], 31; Sheridan and Kisor, "Research Process," 3; Osmer, *Practical Theology*, 48.

5. Silverman, *Doing Qualitative Research*, 9.

6. Berg, *Qualitative Research Methods*, 2; Osmer, *Practical Theology*, 49.

group of charitable organizations in a specific situation and location. Therefore, an in-depth investigation into the philanthropic strategies employed by those organizations and personal lived experiences of the local people involved was thereby required.

The specific methods that I used to collect data were individual and focus group interviews, as well as field notes of my observations as befitting qualitative research.[7] In research, "methods" are techniques that acquire meaning in the context of broader decisions involving how one defines the research problem, database, methods of data analysis, and the researcher's relationship to the subject of her or his study.[8] In this particular case, the research problem was about the ethical aspects of philanthropic strategies employed by charitable organizations such as operated in Mongu and the data sources comprised of human subjects (local community and charitable organizations). It was, therefore, imperative to conduct interviews during the study in order to understand the lived experiences of the people involved or affected by the issue at hand and the meaning that they ascribed to it. As Rick Warren commends, the best way to find out the culture, mindset, and lifestyle of a people is to talk to them.[9]

The study also involved reflexivity, which is literature review in neighboring social sciences such as theology, psychology, sociology, and anthropology in order to establish the meta-theoretical assumptions informing the subject of investigation. That was important for two reasons. First, it helped me as a researcher to read the works of other scholars critically, allowing me to spot background assumptions that provisionally guided the way I carried out my research and performed the respective findings. Second, it also helped me to become more reflexive about my own research. As Richard Osmer, one of the contemporary giants of practical theology from Princeton Theological Seminary writes, research conducted in a community setting requires moving beyond simply getting the information needed to answering the research question and solving the real issue.[10] Therefore, a researcher also needs to determine his or her stance on meta-theoretical issues in dialogue with perspectives currently available by engaging reflexivity in the study.

---

7. Bamberger et al., *RealWorld Evaluation*, 301; Osmer, *Practical Theology*, 61.
8. Seale et al., *Qualitative Research Practice*, 13.
9. Warren, *Purpose Driven Church*, 66.
10. Osmer, *Practical Theology*, 57–58.

## Triangulation

Triangulation in research means examining a phenomenon from multiple perspectives and multiple pieces of data in order to enrich the understanding thereof.[11] As a critical strategy for the credibility of my study for this book, I had to triangulate both the data sources and data collecting methods as recommended by renowned qualitative scholars such as Yvonna S. Lincoln and Egon G. Guba, as well as William Gibson and Andrew Brown.[12]

The different data sources for the research were scheduled interviews with various stakeholders at different times in their geographical locations or naturalistic settings.[13] The different data collection methods were in-depth, one-on-one, face-to-face, semi-structured interviews with "excellent participants" as well as field notes of the researcher's observation.[14] Therefore, triangulation in this case consisted of interviews with various stakeholders and my personal observation in the field of research as well as during the specific interviews.

A key strategy in triangulation is to categorize each group or type of stakeholders in the field of research in order to ensure that the objectives of the research respond to the needs and interests of stakeholders.[15] It was, therefore, imperative for me to ensure inclusion of a comparable number of people from each stakeholder group in the research field so as to enhance validity of the qualitative study.[16] As it were, triangulation in this case was done by looking for outcomes that were agreed upon by all stakeholders. The understanding is that if every stakeholder looking at the issue from a different perspective sees a similar outcome, then the outcome is most likely to be true. In the case study for this book, I ensured inclusion of comparable numbers of participants from senior permanent residents of Mongu district, senior officials of government and charitable organisations (NGOs), as well as gender balance and a cross-section of age groups.

---

11. Nightingale, *Triangulation*, 477; Wilson, *Introducing Research in Nursing*, 84.

12. Lincoln and Guba, *Naturalistic Inquiry*, 305; Gibson and Brown, *Working with Qualitative Data*, 58–59.

13. Gibson and Brown, *Working with Qualitative Data*, 8; Lincoln and Guba, *Naturalistic Inquiry*, 306.

14. An "excellent participant" is one who has been through or personally observed, the experience under investigation. See Bryant and Charmaz, *SAGE Handbook of Grounded Theory*, 231; Bamberger et al., *RealWorld Evaluation*, 301.

15. ICAT, *Sustainable Development Methodology*, 195–96.

16. Guion, *Triangulation*, 1.

Furthermore, my personal observation in the district and during the interviews also formed an integral part of triangulation of the data collection process. As Michael Bamberger and others write, qualitative research involves three hallmark data collection methods, namely observation, interview, and review or analysis of documents or artefacts.[17] Subsequently, the data collection process in the case study included in-depth interviews with qualifying informants as well as field notes of the researcher's observations in the area and during the interviews. As such, the strategy of triangulation also involved the researcher's personal observation in the geographical field of research as well as observation into the interviews in order to provide a thick description of the phenomenon under study. I also made personal notes of my experience during the interview process, observational notes of the participants' verbal and non-verbal expressions, and methodological notes concerning the research process. Such observations during interviews as these also help to explain the actions of participants as they are observed and can also help the researcher to understand the extent to which their statements of intent and beliefs actually inform their behaviour regarding the subject under investigation.[18]

In a broader perspective, I also triangulated data sources throughout the study by means of literature review of various disciplines within social sciences. This helped me to establish the meta-theoretical assumptions informing the study.[19] However, I had to ensure that the influence of theoretical constructions explored in the literature review did not prescribe the theoretical construction of the particular study for this book because the theory of a research must be developed from the research itself.[20]

In a possible summative deduction, triangulation was used for three main purposes, namely, to bolster credibility of the research and data, create a more in-depth picture of the problematic issue at hand, and to investigate different ways of understanding the problem.

Suffice it to extrapolate on the work of this book as a satisfactory qualitative research and its key subsidiaries in the following paragraphs.

---

17. Bamberger et al., *RealWorld Evaluation*, 301.
18. Bamberger et al., *RealWorld Evaluation*, 307.
19. Osmer, *Practical Theology*, 83.
20. Bamberger et al., *RealWorld Evaluation*, 301; Bryant and Charmaz, *SAGE Handbook of Grounded Theory*, 523.

# The Approach

## Qualitative Inquiry

As already mentioned, the study followed qualitative inquiry because it is better suited to studying individuals, groups, or communities in depth.[21] Qualitative research is hereby defined as an iterative process in which improved understanding of the scientific community is achieved by making new significant distinctions resulting from getting closer to the phenomenon being studied.[22] The qualitative research design thus allows for participant's perspectives and understandings of a phenomenon to be revealed as both Sharan Merriam and Michael Patton write.[23] The key concepts in qualitative research are reflexivity, thick description, and naturalism.[24]

The sequence of steps followed in executing the research was according to the general pattern presented by Richard Osmer, namely data collection, data transcription, data analysis and interpretation, and performing research findings.[25] As typical of qualitative inquiry, no fixed sample size was determined beforehand because the interviews had to be conducted until data saturation occurred.[26] As it were, prefixing a restrictive timeframe was also inhibited by the availability of informants that could not be guaranteed at first approach as well as budget, time, and political constraints, which are also not uncommon issues with qualitative inquiries.[27]

As a qualitative inquiry, the case study had explorative, descriptive, and contextual foci in order to get closer to and acquire in-depth understanding of the ethical aspects of philanthropic strategies that were employed by charitable organizations in Mongu district and, by default, in Zambia.

## Explorative Approach

Explorative research in social sciences implies a broad-range, purposive, scientific, and pre-arranged undertaking designed to optimize

---

21. Osmer, *Practical Theology*, 50.
22. Aspers and Corte, "What Is Qualitative," 1.
23. Cf. Anfara and Metz, *Theoretical Frameworks*, 34.
24. Gibson and Brown, *Working with Qualitative Data*, 8.
25. Osmer, *Practical Theology*, 55–57.
26. Borg et al., *Applying Educational Research*, 101; Parse et al., "Nursing Research," 18.
27. Bamberger et al., *RealWorld Evaluation*, 6–10.

generalizations that can lead to a detailed description and understanding of an area of social or psychological life.[28] According to Richard Swedberg and Norman Blaikie, an explorative research is undertaken when very little is known about the subject being investigated or about the context in which the research is to be conducted.[29] This means that the topic may have never been investigated at all or at least not in that particular context. The aim of exploratory research is to discover the relationships and dimensions of a phenomenon.[30]

In this particular case, the need to explore arose from the scarcity of specific documented information regarding the subject under investigation. Furthermore, the study is considered to have been explorative because it sought to understand the local people's experiences of the ethicality of philanthropic strategies implemented by charitable organizations in their area and the meaning that they ascribed to it. As an explorative researcher, I also endeavored to establish facts and collect new data in order to determine if there were any interesting patterns or regularities in the data as Walter Borg et al. and Johann Mouton write.[31] Said another way, the study aimed to explore the ethical aspects of philanthropic strategies that were employed by charitable organizations operating in Mongu district of Western Zambia and determine whether the data collected revealed certain common patterns and regularities as well as if they disclosed some specific relationships that attracted research attention.

## Descriptive Approach

The aim of the descriptive approach in the study was to provide an in-depth or thick description of the philanthropic strategies of charitable organizations such as operated among poor African communities such as in Mongu district of Western Zambia, and develop action-guiding concepts to enhance their ethicality, based on findings of the data that was collected. As a descriptive study, the process involved attending to the words and actions

---

28. Stebbins, *Exploratory Research*, 3.

29. Swedberg, *On the Uses of Exploratory Research*, 1–5; Blaikie, *Designing Social Research*, 73.

30. Talbot, *Principles and Practice*, 90.

31. Borg et al., *Applying Educational Research*, 195; Mouton, *Understanding Social Research*, 103.

of the people involved or concerned without filtering them through interpretive and normative judgments.[32]

It is, however, important to note that the descriptive approach in this sense was not inference-free, but rather a methodological approach of least inference among categories of qualitative work.[33] In accordance with the just quoted author in the footnote, the fundamental concern of a descriptive approach is to provide a sort of report of events, institutional structures, and commonly observable behaviors, as well as the meaning of these things for the people studied. As such, there must be at least a conscious movement of acknowledging the phenomenon under study in order to come up with a valid description of the reality.

In view of the foregoing, the descriptive approach in the work of this book is considered to be flexible, iterative, and naturalistic so as to result in thick descriptions that are flexible in ways in which the research data was constructed.[34] Although many a study do portray descriptive elements as a whole, this research design would, in accordance with Earl Barbie and Johann Mouton, as well as Michael Sheridan and Anne Kisor, endeavor as much as possible to break down the whole into smaller segments that could be studied in details.[35]

## Contextual Approach

"Context" hereby means the physical, geographical, cultural, historical or aesthetic setting within which action takes place as the American sociologist Sara Lawrence-Lightfoot writes.[36] It is fundamentally preferable that a research is conducted within its specific context because conceptual validity is only achieved when both the constructs of investigation and any philosophical assumptions drawn from there are acknowledged and understood within the context of their study.[37] As such, it is both logically and

---

32. Osmer, *Practical Theology*, 59; Sandelowski, "What Is in a Name?," 77–84.
33. Seixas et al., "Qualitative Descriptive Approach," 779.
34. Gibson and Brown, *Working with Qualitative Data*, 7.
35. Barbie and Mouton, *Practice of Social Research*, 53; Sheridan and Kisor, "Research Process and the Elderly," 102.
36. Cf. Patton, *Qualitative Research and Evaluation Methods*, 63.
37. Knight et al., "Context and Contextual Constructs," 7.

scientifically acceptable to infer that human nature is specified and made intelligible by the particular context in which it is found.[38]

Therefore, the ethical aspects of philanthropic strategies employed by charitable organizations in Mongu district and Zambia were thereby investigated within the context where they existed in order to understand the surrounding dynamics and systems.[39] Accordingly, the study gathered detailed data pertaining to the topic under study as revealed in its unique and naturalistic context. I then developed and described action-guiding concepts for enhancing ethicality of philanthropic strategies by the charities in Mongu district and Zambia as a country because the issue that was being addressed concerned not only the town of Mongu, but the country of Zambia as whole and Africa at large as revealed by the literature survey.

Although the research findings are hereby valid within the specific time, space, and value context, Nancy Burns and Susan Grove observe that by understanding the meaning of a phenomenon in its context, it becomes rather easier to understand phenomena in other similar situations.[40]

## Ethical Considerations

It is cardinal to recognize that all projects involving human subjects are increasingly being subjected to ethical scrutiny in recent years with most professional associations, funders, and even universities demanding that any such project or study receives ethical approval before it is carried out.[41] The reason for such heightened ethical critique as this is to minimize the negative consequences of such projects on individuals and societies.[42] As such, the research for this book was conducted in an ethically acceptable and feasible manner.[43]

Generally, a project is considered to be ethically acceptable if the inherent risks are reasonable in relation to the potential benefits to the participants, both directly and indirectly.[44] As such, a risk-benefit analysis

38. Schwandt, *Qualitative Inquiry*, 37.
39. Schurink, "Deciding to Use," 281.
40. Botes, "Functional Approach," 22; Burns and Grove, *Practice of Nursing Research*, 29.
41. Sapsford and Jupp, *Data Collection and Analysis*, 293.
42. Bamberger et al., *RealWorld Evaluation*, 170.
43. Marshall and Rossman, *Designing Qualitative Research*, 82.
44. TRREE, *Introduction to Research Ethics*, 25.

THE APPROACH

was executed to further minimize the risk and ensure that the benefits of the study to the participants clearly outweighed the risks. According to the risk-benefit analysis conducted, the risks were reasonably minimal in relation to the benefits to participants and the overall benefits of the work clearly outweigh the risks.

As such, the work of this publication is considered to be of negligible risk because it is designed to enhance ethical operational strategies and professionalism of charitable organizations and optimize benefits to the local community. The study was thus approved by the University of South Bohemia in České Budějovice as meeting acceptable ethical standards.

Notwithstanding the negligible risk level of the study, I still note with caution that the study also borders on the moral integrity of charitable organizations, an aspect that might be considered as threatening to expose the participating organizations, but that is not the aim of this book.

Furthermore, a project or study should have both social value and scientific validity or rigor in order to be considered viable as enshrined in the Training and Resources in Research Ethics Evaluation (TRREE) manual developed by the Clinical Trials Centre at the University of Hong Kong.[45] In order to have social value, the just cited source underwrites that a project should be designed to solve a problem that is relevant to community concerns or has been identified by the community as a problem that needs to be addressed. As earlier mentioned in the background contextual and core issues, the problem that prompted the work of this book is the fact that next to nothing was known about the ethical obligations and operating strategies of charitable organizations in Mongu town and country of Zambia at large. Furthermore, the quality of life of the people in the communities had not improved despite an influx of charitable organizations in the area for at least a century. And sadly so, at least 80 percent of the people in Mongu still lived below the poverty datum line. My physical inquiry at the Ministry of Community Development and Social Services[46] revealed that even the government was concerned and yet to establish the relevant details about the nature and work of charitable organizations in the communities. It is, therefore, inferred that this book has social value.

Equally, this book is also considered to be scientifically valid because it has potential to result in facts, reproducible observations or generalizable

---

45. TRREE, *Introduction to Research Ethics*, 8.
46. MCDSS, *NGO File 2018*, 1, 7–9.

information that relate to the subject under study.[47] As the just cited source in the footnote further states, in qualitative research, instead of scientific validity only, a researcher should strive to achieve scientific rigour as well. As revealed earlier in the background contextual issues, the problematic praxis with ethical aspects of philanthropic strategies employed by charitable organizations applies not only to the community of Mongu, but also to other national and global contexts. Therefore, there is need for a scientifically rigorous evaluation of the subject under investigation in order to shape philanthropic activities of charitable organizations towards desirable ends.

In addition and as a rule of the thumb, the study adhered to all standard ethical considerations such as informed consent, confidentiality and anonymity, respect and trust, as well as honest disclosure of research findings.

I am, therefore, under the impression that this book will also contribute to the understanding of philanthropic social work with regard to ethics in charity from an indigenous African context and the charitable organizations operating therein. As already alluded to, understanding the meaning of a phenomenon in its context also enhances understanding of phenomena in other similar situations because particular system are nestled within other systems in the broader web of life.

## Summary Perspectives on the Approach

The approach to the problematic issue regarding ethical aspects of philanthropic strategies employed by charitable organizations operating among poor African communities has so far been presented in this chapter. The main features of the approach are the strategy of inquiry, which is qualitative, and the specific techniques involved that include interviews, observations, and review of artefacts. Triangulations was imperative in order to ensure credibility of the study. As a qualitative inquiry, the study had explorative, descriptive, and contextual foci. Finally, the ethical considerations made during the research process have also been presented to bolster credibility of the work of this book.

The next chapter shows the workings as it comprises the research results and actual evaluation of ethical aspects of philanthropic strategies employed by charitable organizations.

47. TRREE, *Introduction to Research Ethics*, 8.

# 5

# Showing the Workings

## INTRODUCTION

This chapter shows the workings of the research by focusing on the empirical research results of the case study and actual evaluation of the ethical aspects of philanthropic strategies employed by charitable organizations in Mongu district of Western Zambia, whereby the praxis could be observed and explained. Semi-structured interviews were conducted with government officials of the concerned sectors, leading officials of concerned NGOs, and senior citizens who had lived in Mongu for at least five years, among whom were women and youths. The interviews with government and NGO officials were conducted as one-on-one, face-to-face conversations, while those with senior citizens took the form of both one-on-one and focus group face-to-face discussions.

Not to bore the reader with all my academic jargon, I will provide only a succinct discussion and interpretation of the research findings from the interviews conducted with participants in order to reveal the ethical aspects implicit in the philanthropic strategies employed by charitable organizations. The implicit ethical aspects are then evaluated against relevant ethical theories and later (in chapter 6) discussed together with theoretical concepts from the wider research in order to bridge the perceived gap between theory and practice in the formulation of a new praxis and model to guide the ethical evaluation of philanthropic strategies by charitable organizations.[1]

---

1. Payne, *Modern Social Work Theory*, 4.

The study was conducted in its contextual uniqueness and would, therefore, help the local community and other stakeholders to discover perspectives that could be descriptive-empirical evidence of the ethical aspects at stake in the execution of philanthropic strategies employed by the charitable organizations and thus come up with a model that aspires to evaluate such aspects as revealed. According to Nancy Burns and Susan Grove, this will also assist to understand similar phenomena in other contexts.[2]

## DISCUSSION AND INTERPRETATION OF RESEARCH RESULTS

Discussion and interpretation of research results are in this respect for the purpose of understanding, rather than explanation. According to Bamberger and others, a deep contextual understanding of the particular phenomenon is the goal of qualitative inquiry.[3] It is, therefore, not merely an abstract understanding, but such as is "deeply, personally felt," as the just cited co-authors observe. Suffice it to highlight the fact that interpretation is among the most important aspects of research as it leads a researcher to delve deeper into the issue and come out with a wider perspective beyond just his experience.[4] As such, this section concentrates on providing a detailed analysis of the data collected by presenting sufficient and accurate thick descriptions of the ethical aspects of philanthropic strategies employed by charitable organizations, so as to understand patterns and dynamics that can be isolated from or identified with others in the broader spectrum of discourse and research. Personal experiences of the respondents and field observations of the researcher equally formed integral parts of the data analysis and presentation.

The method of operation is discussed first, in order to ensure transparency, and then the research results will be explored. Theory regarding sampling, the pilot study, and semi-structured interviews have already been discussed. As such, only the results of the interviews and discussions thereof are presented in this chapter.

---

2. Burns and Grove, *Practice of Nursing Research*, 29.
3. Bamberger et al., *RealWorld Evaluation*, 293.
4. Struwig and Stead, *Planning, Designing, and Reporting*, 552.

Note that only results of the interviews conducted by the researcher are discussed at this stage, conclusions are made later. The respective results are hereafter presented in form of themes.

## Theme 1: Reasons for Failure by Charitable Organizations to Make Impact in the Community

An overwhelming view was held by all participants in the research that the charitable organizations failed to make any positive impact in the community so far. The participants cited several reasons for the failure, some of which were related to the social and cultural characteristics of the local people, while others were related to the operational praxis of the NGOs in the respective communities. Above all, most of the reasons cited border on sensitive ethical issues regarding philanthropic strategies employed by charitable organizations and this calls for ethical reflection with universal ethical principles. In an interview, one of the participants lamented that NGOs were just using people to their own advantage: "They are just using us to enrich themselves. Nothing is happening!"

Outrightly, the dignity and worth of the human person and other ethical aspects were being violated in this case! Several other participants expressed sentiments that raise questions regarding the ethicality of the charitable organizations as hereafter sampled out.

### *Reasons Related to Social-Cultural Aspects*

Reasons related to the social-cultural aspects of the people of Mongu include local indigenous people not being supportive to their own land and people in the execution of philanthropic strategies by charitable organizations operating in the town. Some participants highlighted particular subversive aspects such as ignorance, greed, jealous, and tribalism as having contributed to the failure by the charities to impact the community positively. To some extent, one might rationalize that it is due to such reasons that even some of the well-to-do indigenous people opted to move out or invest elsewhere outside their home town. The question arises as to what extent culture has influence on philanthropy and development. Such reasons as categorized under this theme seriously undermine ethical aspects like good practice, practical moral reasoning, and respect for diversities.

## Indigenous Employees of Charitable Organizations Not Fair to Their Homeland and People

The participants observed that the indigenous local people employed by charitable organizations were not fair to their own people in the distribution of charitable goods and services as per the following sample quote: "Maybe, it's just an appeal to these organizations—the people on the ground, they're the ones that don't do the right thing.... They're there to disadvantage their own people, their own kids."

## Poor Working Cultures of Both Local People and Charitable Organizations

Some participants also observed that the working culture of both the local people and charitable organizations were rather inhibiting the smooth and ethical operations of NGOs as per the following excerpts from respondents:

i. To some extent there's the cultural aspect. To be specific... I've seen that there's a lot of protocol to be observed in this place. So, even NGOs are not expanding.... I think that's the major hindrance for me. The cultural aspect.

ii. Even charitable organizations ... I don't know, maybe it's just the culture or, but again there're quite a lot of factors that could have contributed to the, you know, the poor, you know, working culture of charity work in Mongu district.

According to one participant, it is also possible that some charitable organizations failed to make impact in the broader traditional African communities because they worked outside the confines of the local people's culture.

> I also think that NGOs especially here in Africa, they don't pay much attention to our culture, our cultural norms and everything that pertains to our traditions. So, somehow, they seem to contradict, they seem to contradict certain cultural norms. So, I feel they should try to work within the confines of culture, that's the certain type of culture that they find in the area where they operate.

## Tribalism

Africa in general has faced problems of getting people with different tribal, ethnic, cultural, and religious backgrounds to live together in peace and harmony in a just, participatory, and sustainable society.[5] Most of the participants that I personally interviewed mentioned tribalism as a negative factor that hindered smooth progress of the charitable organizations. Here is a sample quote: "We're part of Zambia, but you find that there's this burning issue of tribal lines."

Like racism, tribalism is a violation of fundamental human rights as it results in unequal opportunities in critical human developmental aspects like education and employment, lack of cooperation among members of the local communities, as well as unfair treatment before the law. For poor people to effectively penetrate the NGO structures and get help, they need to find a way to balance "self-help and mutual help," and tribalism can be a big threat in this regard. Poor people will have to consider options like cooperatives as a way to pull their little resources together in order to promote their common welfare.

Some participants observed that employment opportunities by charitable organizations were also offered on tribal basis and not necessarily as equal opportunity employers to ethically empower local people.

## *Reasons Related to Operational Praxis.*

The following reasons as provided in the responses by participants are related to the operational praxis of charitable organizations that operated in Mongu.

## Lack of Continuity / Sustainability

Most participants seemed to realize that continuity is an integral part of success and sustainability as they cited lack of continuity as a major reason for failure by charitable organizations to make positive impact in the community. The activities and efforts of charitable organizations are seen to be disjointed and short-lived, thus unsustainable and without impact in the community. Sustainability is the maintenance and continuance of

---

5. Adeyemo, *Africa Bible Commentary*, 1425.

economic and social development projects in various communities.[6] Therefore, sustainability of any community project also inextricably depends on community participation in the project planning, implementation, and decision-making. Good practice as an ethical norm is at stake in this case. During the interviews, one of the participants elaborated explicitly on this aspect and several others echoed similar sentiments. This appeals to ethical aspects such as good practice and the following verbatim excerpt says it all:

> I also noticed changes, there are new faces from time to time. Some people go and others come in. . . . I noticed that there are few people who live here permanently and are always active here. . . . So, whatever we do, we do it with proportionate, fare, symmetrical, local development towards sustainability. Basically, what we do, after we're gone the result should be well aligned, so well aligned with the local systems that the people should be able to work with it sustainably and it should be so well integrated into the local system because these are things of the local society. It should be in the fibres of the society so that it will continue being utilized and being developed by the local people.

### Personal Gain and Misappropriation of Charitable Resources

> Those that are championing NGOship have become so greedy. Maybe they're using the name of NGOs to . . . put food on their table![7]

The ethicality of philanthropic strategies by NGOs was compromised by the self-centered actions of NGO officials that were aimed at improving their own economic status at the expense of the larger community. The participants described the aspirations of the different role players to achieve personal gain or individual agenda as another reason for the failure of NGOs to impact the community positively and bring about the desired social economic transformation. In understanding these destructive actions and aspirations, one needs to note that a lack of good planning, leadership and understanding of philanthropic strategies could greatly have contributed to a situation where those entrusted with donor resources rather used them for themselves than channeling them to the rightful end users. A lack

---

6. Abiche, "Community Development Initiatives," 27.
7. Sample response from an anonymous respondent.

of strong leadership and clear direction, especially in conditions of great poverty and need, might further motivate people to "take" what they can. Critical ethical aspects such as social justice, equality and fairness, as well as transparency and accountability are seriously at stake in this case.

An opinion was held by some participants that NGOs that got money from outside the country were diverting the help to their own personal interests, while local NGOs struggled to get help, even when their intentions were genuine. For example, a respondent is hereby cited as follows:

> But the worst kind of NGO operatives that we have seen are those that are getting help outside the country, which is coming in this country. It's not going to the recipients—the people that it is meant for. It is coming to me. . . . But for the local ones, it's a, it's a sorry sight. They struggle to get help. Yeah, they struggle to get help, even though their intentions are genuine, but I think sourcing of funds has been a problem.

## Duplicity of Activities

Uncoordinated philanthropic efforts by NGOs are most likely to bring about duplicity of activities to either same people or same places, or both. This is the case of helping the *nearest* instead of the *neediest*, which is unethical because the nearest is not always the neediest. This also is inimical to good practice and triggers the obvious ethical question of the deserving and undeserving poor. Both NGO and non-NGO officials who willingly participated in the interviews alluded to the fact that there was duplicity of philanthropic activities in the communities due to lack of coordination among the NGOs themselves. As an example one of the respondents had the following to say:

> One of the biggest problems I've always had is there's duplicity, I don't know if that's the correct term. You will find that there's this lack of coordination, where you find two, three, four NGOs basically doing the same thing, and so with little impact. So, you think that if they were well coordinated, then we don't have to have five, six, NGOs, three, NGOs, four NGOs doing the same thing. It's duplicated effort, yeah.

Most of the charitable organizations focused on the same areas, especially the more accessible urbanized areas while the far flung remote areas were neglected.

## Overdependence on External Support

It became evident from the interviews also that most charitable organizations relied entirely on external support, which was not sustainable: "So, as a result, local organizations that are in charity work get affected because they entirely depend on donor support." Instead of depending totally on external donor aid, the local communities ought to identify their needs and design their path to economic growth and transformation with minimal external influence and support where needed. Suffice it to restate that external philanthropic aid should be managed in such a way that it will not disempower local initiatives and cause dependency. The ethical issue at stake here is that of *dependency* verses *self-determination*. So, the focus should be on increasing self-reliance, such as through income generating initiatives.[8] In this regard, the local community is expected to utilize philanthropic support to help individuals and communities to attain sustainable transformational development through technical, physical, and financial support to enhance bigger and long term transformational projects as Hoek and Yardley observe.[9]

## Lack of Effective Monitoring and Evaluation of Charitable Organizations

As it were, Zambia as a country had no policy to govern or monitor NGOs from precolonial times and that was what actually prompted me to undertake the study leading to this publication as earlier stated. It was, therefore, not known to what extent the ethical obligations of the said NGOs were honored or dishonored in the implementation of their philanthropic strategies. Now, that is a serious lapse in terms of transparency and accountability of the NGOs. Apparently, some participants in the interviews also alluded to lack of monitoring and evaluation of NGOs as a contributing factor to the failure by the said organizations to make positive impact.

---

8. Blackman, *Partnering with the Local Church*, 30.
9. Hoek and Yardley, *Keeping Communities Clean*, 6.

> Who monitors the charity, you know, work of these organizations in the district? Quite alright we have community development, but again also they're in charge this time around they're telling you, no, you should register with us, do that, but at the end of the day, do they have also capacity to monitor or hold accountable you know the charitable organizations?

Said another way, there were not checks and balances, which is a critical ethical issue!

## Lack of Skills and Understanding of Philanthropic Strategies

A lack of skills and understanding of philanthropic strategies is directly implied as a reason for the failure of the charities to impact the community positively. This shortfall is further associated with not understanding the true needs of the people, which results into projects that seem to be imposed on the people and this is met by failure to make impact. A respondent is hereby cited saying: :

> Generally, overall, I'd say NGOs usually come with their own predefined, or predetermined idea. . . . So, you may find, these are services or support services that are more, NGO driven, and not necessary community driven. So they seem to be imposed on the people. So, when services like that are imposed, then we have a problem. They tend to have little acceptance from the people.

Again the ethic of good practice hereby arises.

It also became evident that the local charities did not have the skills to work with external experts to ensure that their philanthropic strategies addressed the real pressing needs of the local people in the communities.

## Corruption

Corruption "sands the wheels of development in Africa" as it negatively compromises ethics such as integrity, transparency, accountability, equality, and fairness, among others.[10] The participants highlighted that the aspect of corruption was very serious among charitable organizations: "The issue of corruption is very serious there. We're killed by what? Corruption! That's

---

10. Owoye and Bissessar, "Bad Governance and Corruption in Africa," 1.

what is killing us. If there are some people who can talk to them on corruption, let them go and talk to them. . . . What is there is corruption!"

Suffice it to also highlight that it is critical for charitable organizations to understand the complexity of donor aid from a broader perspective when engaging in charitable activities in the communities. If not used properly and at the proper time, aid can breed corruption, dependency, and even encourage violent tensions.[11]

### Tension with Government / Political Influence

Cooperation with government in implementing charitable activities can be either a positive contribution or negative hindrance, especially when donor aid is involved. The government and politicians have their own agenda, which may not necessarily be aligned to that of some charitable organizations and donors. Critical decisions have to be made amidst ethical dilemmas of whether to follow government dictates or stick to the terms of reference of a given charity as some respondents also observed:

> Sometimes even just political influence has contributed to poor working culture of charitable organizations. . . . Yeah, so those politics also sometimes influence where the money should be, where the resources should be going.

As such, good practice and practical moral reasoning such as careful planning and consideration is required when engaging government and politicians in the process of implementing philanthropic strategies by charitable organizations. Otherwise, there is likely to be tensions and frictions between government and charitable organizations.

### Uncoordinated and insufficient efforts

The participants identified interventions by some charitable organizations that were beneficial to the community in terms of supplementing government efforts and other assorted community aspects. These interventions addressed a range of needs from education, nutritional support, to HIV/AIDS and Covid-19 preventive and relief measures. From the interviews, however, it seemed that those were not necessarily coordinated proactive philanthropic efforts that could have a remarkable positive impact in the

---

11. Ayodele et al., *African Perspectives on Aid*, 1–2; Collier, *Bottom Billion*, 106.

community. This is evident from the amount of duplicity of activities mentioned in the statements of the participants. The said efforts also could not be described as sufficient to cause positive impact in the community. The issue that seems to come to the fore is that of temporary relief (dependence) versus permanent change (self-sustaining).

## Theme 2: True Needs of the People

Key to implementation of effective philanthropic strategies is accurate understanding of the real pressing problems and felt needs of the target population or community.[12] During the interviews, participants revealed their real pressing problems and felt needs as hereafter presented. Apparently, all the community problems and needs identified by the participants were directly associated with the Sustainable Development Goals (SDGs) as outlined by the United Nations.[13] Therefore, ethical philanthropy in this case should aim at noble causes such as eliminating poverty, empowering communities, social justice, deserving poor, and, in the broader sense, ethical reflection with universal ethical principles.

### Poverty

No poverty, zero hunger, and good health and wellbeing are the first three of the seventeen global Sustainable Development Goals as per United Nations target.[14] Suffice it to highlight that poverty is a strong determinant of other human problems.[15] Accordingly, poverty contributes to several human problems such as physical weakness through lack of food, small bodies, malnutrition leading to low immune response to infectious diseases, and inability to reach or pay for health services. It also contributes to isolation due to inability to pay the cost of education, recreation, travelling to find work, live near the village centre or main road. Ethically, charitable activities should fundamentally aim to eliminate poverty, as a pre-requisite to effectively address other connected human problems. In my empirical research, participants identified poverty as a major problem to an extent

---

12. Gautier, "Building a Philanthropic Strategy."
13. UNDSDG, "Seventeen Goals."
14. UNDSDG, "Seventeen Goals."
15. Swanepoel and Beer, *Community Development*, 111.

that some members of the community could not even afford enough food for themselves and their families as per the following sample quote:

> The most pressing need is poverty. Poverty is much more on the higher side. It has impacted negatively on the livelihoods of many people. For example, quite a good number of boys and girls you find them loitering on the streets. Hunger is number one on the list!

According to the third SDG, everybody has a right to good health and well-being, but poverty happens to be a big hindrance in this regard.

*Lack of Employment and Empowerment*

Employment and empowerment are synonymous in terms of impacting the socio-economic life of a people as they are both critical to local and global success.[16] According to SDG 8, *decent work and economic growth* is everybody's right.[17] As such, where there are no employment opportunities, other forms of empowerment such as skills development and other income generating initiatives should provide alternative livelihoods of similar or even higher quality for a people. For instance, one participant in my research interviews said: "Empowerment! We're a country going into the phase where we have realized that the best way to reduce unemployment is to let people employ themselves." Apparently, some people such as interviewed in my research found themselves in a predicament of being without either employment or empowerment opportunities. As a result, young people resorted to bad vices such as prostitution for girls and criminal activities for boys. Ethically, philanthropy should aim at noble causes such as empowering individuals and communities, healing injustices and overcoming unjust policies. In a broader perspective, again ethical reflection with universal ethical principles also comes into consideration in this regard.

Specifically, there is critical need for empowerment among the people in local communities, especially women and youths, to prevent negative vices such as gender-based violence and the prevalence of street kids, among others.

---

16. UNDESA, "Youth Education."
17. UNDSDG, "Seventeen Goals."

## Transport and Communication

Transport and communication challenges due to poor road infrastructure and mobile phone networks were cited among the major problems that people in rural areas face.

> The road network is not okay, we need to improve on our roads. So, I'll say transport and just general communication. And you find these are areas where even the network providers, the network signals are not strong enough for them to be able to call for help when they need it.

Consequently, some sectors of community were unable to access basic services such as health and education. Ethical giving should address such critical basic aspects of human survival as these.

## Education

This is another noble cause for ethical philanthropy. One of the necessary preconditions for transforming Africa's poorest communities is having a larger percentage of the respective population attain the prerequisite education.[18] According to the United Nations Conference on Trade and Development, there is need for inclusive developmental programmes that provide for better access to education, especially for the poor, increase the economy's stock of human capital and thus have a positive impact on community growth and productivity.[19] The people who participated in my research seemed to be aware of critical needs in the education sector in their community as, just as an example, one respondent is cited saying, "There's definitely huge, dire needs in the education sector." Ignorance is hereby perceived as a lack of education and negative vice against development, which raises the need to adequately educate the community populace.

## Health

To every human being, health comes first. As such, ethical philanthropy should also prioritise human health. As Abubakar Yahaya and Ali Gunduz rightly observe, the protection and enhancement of good health is the

---

18. Collier, *Bottom Billion*, 70–71.
19. Cf. Osakwe and Poretti, *Trade and Poverty Alleviation*, 3.

highest blessing any human being needs.[20] Therefore, inclusive developmental programs that promote better access to good health services, especially for the poor, and increase the economy's stock of human capital have a positive impact on community growth and transformation.[21] The participants indicated that there were a lot of health related problems that needed to be addressed in their communities. "There are huge needs in the health sector." For instance, water and sanitation were some of the highlighted health related issues.

*Climate Change*

This is also in line with one of the SDGs, namely Climate Action—SDG 13.[22] Climate change disproportionately affects the continent of Africa, especially in the agricultural sector.[23] Therefore, preservation of the ecosystem and sustainable utilization of natural resources is an ethical obligation of every human person on earth. As such, giving for climate change intervention is ethically acceptable. Some participants in my research also seemed to be aware of the effects of climate change on their valuable natural resources such as water bodies and fish species. Take for instance the following quote from a respondent:

> The real pressing issues, let me speak in particular to Western Province, per se; issues of climate change. . . . Climate change has been a pressing issue because, even when you see our water bodies, the fish is depleting. Where are we going? These are the issues that have been brought about by climate change. Yeah, so, we have issues of climate change here. It's really affected the province in particular.

Furthermore, human survival activities such as indiscriminate cutting of trees exacerbated the effects that climate change already had on the region and the participants realized that was a real pressing problem and, actually, a priority concern.

---

20. Yahaya and Gunduz, "Importance of Healthy Human Life," 63.
21. Osakwe and Poretti, *Trade and Poverty Alleviation*, 3.
22. UNDSDG, "Seventeen Goals."
23. Ngaira, "Impact of Climate Change," 238–43.

## Theme 3: Strategies Employed by Charitable Organizations

Two extremely opposing views were held regarding the strategies employed by charitable organizations operating among the respective local communities and, apparently, each extreme view was raised and supported by an interested party. On one hand, the participants from the local community and government expressed ignorance about the strategies employed by the said NGOs, with some at most indicating that the NOGs were biased and irrational in their strategies. A respondent said, "I don't know what criteria they use because you still find a lot of those people who need their services on the street, and they cannot be taken on. So, you start to think and to say then what are they doing?"

On the other hand, officials of charitable NGOs themselves mentioned a handful of strategies that they employed in the discharge of their philanthropic activities, including supporting and networking with oversight government ministries or departments and other stakeholders, community sensitization, and capacity building in form of training workshops.

Most of the charitable organizations were also connected to some churches in one way or another, a scenario that can be described as remarkable from the point of view of ethics as churches are supposed to uphold high moral standards. Furthermore, most of the charitable NGOs staff that I interviewed appealed to the aspect of Christian spirituality to enhance success in the execution of their philanthropic strategies. This is probably because of their connection with the church and the declaration of Zambia as a Christian nation. The following quote from a respondent is a typical example in this case:

> I think as an organization as I've said it's an NGO and at the same time it's a faith-based organization. So, we have some Christian values of course, where we normally inculcate those Christian values in the people that we're working with. . . . We ensure that in our issues we bring in the issues of spiritual aspects, because we know that even to change certain mind-sets, we need spiritual intervention. . . . So, even when we go into the communities, in whatever we do we need to put God first—prayer and other things.

A big question, however, is whether the strategies described by participants representing NGOs addressed the true needs of the local people as expressed in the previous section. This is an ethical question! Ethical reflection with universal ethical principles, good practice, and practical moral reasoning are directly implicit in this case, too. An observation is hereby made that most of the strategies that the NGOs claimed to employ did not address the true needs, which were the real pressing problems and felt needs of the local people as expressed in the previous section, a scenario that is not in tandem with ethics in philanthropy. This is probably why the local people who were not part of the charitable NGOs expressed ignorance about the philanthropic strategies employed by the charitable organisations in their communities.

## Theme 4: Expectations Regarding Charitable Organizations.

In general, the participants expected charitable organizations to do a lot more than what they were currently doing in order to bring about positive impact in the communities. In particular, they expected NGOs to uplift living standards of the people, supplement government efforts, coordinate themselves properly, and cover both urban and far flung rural areas.

> We're not that productive after many years of NGOs which aim to make the people's livelihoods improve, which are supposed to make the people self-employed, which are supposed to make the people small time businessmen. . . . So, if you had something that would give the people viable livelihoods, where they can look after themselves, they can start producing as microeconomic units. I think that's what we're looking for because they'll be tied to that which is giving them jobs since there's no one who can give those jobs.

Furthermore, participants also expected NGOs operating in their communities to be monitored and evaluated, practical and true, help vulnerable members of the community, understand the communities through community research, and help with capacity building in the communities. It is also remarkable that the people's expectations were connected to their true needs, an aspect that the charitable organizations should take into serious consideration.

Philanthropic ethics connected with the people's expectations are ethical reflection with universal ethical principles, social justice, integrity, good practice, transparency and accountability, as well as the aspect of deserving and undeserving poor people. As it were, the goals of charity in developing countries are to help communities rebuild, advance, become sustainable, and eliminate social and economic inequality.[24] According to their expectations, the local people seem to possess this understanding and, therefore, charitable organizations should engage them in identifying their true needs and strategizing the way out with them.

## Summary of Descriptive-Empirical Perspectives from the Case Study

The empirical case study investigated the praxis and ethicality of philanthropic strategies employed by charitable organizations such as operated in Mongu town of Western Zambia. There was overwhelming response that the charitable organizations failed to make positive impact in the community and the participants cited several reason for the failure, some related to socio-cultural aspects of the local people, while others related to operational practices of the charitable organizations themselves. The research also unearthed the true needs of the local community, as well as the strategies employed by the said charities, which apparently did not seem to address the real pressing needs of the target communities.

Suffice it to highlight that poverty is a strong determinant of other human problems such as physical weakness through lack of food, small bodies, malnutrition leading to low immune response to infectious diseases, and inability to reach or pay for health services and education, among others. Finally, the research revealed several expectations of the local people regarding charitable organizations and, as it were, their expectations are inextricably linked to their true needs.

In no particular order, the ethical implications of the foregoing research findings are: ethical reflection with universal ethical principles, social justice, respect for diversities, dignity and worth of the human person, good practice, practical moral reasoning, equality and fairness, transparency and accountability, integrity, self-determination, sustainability, ethical dilemmas, giving for noble causes, and the question of deserving and undeserving poor people. As stated in the introduction to this chapter, these ethical aspects will be evaluated against relevant ethical theories in the next section, and then discussed together with other concepts emerging from the wider research in the next chapter in order to bridge the perceived gap between theory and practice, which in this case pertains to evaluating ethical aspects of philanthropic strategies by charitable organizations.

24. Burgess-Van Aken, "Goals of Philanthropy."

## Member Checking

For those interested in some academic jargon, member checking is the review of a researcher's interpretations by participants representing the relevant stakeholders in order to verify the findings.[25] Participants are thus charged with responsibility of confirming or disconfirming the reasonableness of the interpretations drawn from the data by the researcher so that corrections could be made if need be.

Accordingly, the empirical research findings for the work of this book as well as the preliminary interpretations drawn from them were presented to several community representatives who participated in the research interviews for the specific purpose of member checking.[26] In some cases, I sent the research results and interpretations electronically to individual participants whom I could not physically reach so that they could also give their feedback. Apparently, all the participants engaged in member checking confirmed that the interpretations were appropriate.

The foregoing ethical aspects will now be evaluated against relevant ethical theories to develop a robust and coherent argument for the ethical evaluation of philanthropic strategies employed by charitable organizations.

## ETHICAL EVALUATION

Real science requires that there should be some rational connection between explanatory theory and empirical data.[27] For instance, it can be argued from the viewpoint of critical realism that empirical research alone does not offer direct access to natural and social objects and phenomena, because it does not answer the 'why' question. As Richard Osmer observes, empirical research should rather interact with theory in testing, revising, and elaborating its perspectives so as to understand why things are happening in a particular way in a given situation and context.[28] It is this interaction of empirical research and theory that leads to the formulation of more adequate explanations of the natural and social worlds.

From an interpretive social science perspective, social science and theory are a form of practice and are essentially ethics in part. In their

---

25. Bamberger et al., *RealWorld Evaluation*, 139.
26. Gabriel, *Human Factor in Rural Development*, 110.
27. Murphy, *Reasoning and Rhetoric*, 13.
28. Osmer, *Practical Theology*, 71.

article "Interpretive Social Science: An Overview," Frank Richardson and Blaine Fowers claim that social science and theory are an extension of our search for justice, love, and wisdom in a practical real life situation.[29] Accordingly, the co-authors are of the view that an interpretive social science or hermeneutical approach offers a relatively coherent view of social inquiry that helps a researcher to incorporate the virtues and avoid the limitations of other perspectives. In accordance with this theoretical perspective too, I have selectively and purposefully drawn on theories that are relevant to ethical philanthropy as it relates to the topic under study rather than just fit things into any theory.

## Ethical Theoretical Perspectives

The identified ethical theories are implicit both from empirical research and relevant to enriching our understanding of ethical aspects of philanthropic strategies employed by charitable organizations from a broader theoretical perspective, which is also consistent with Osmer's observation too.[30] Furthermore, the discussion of the identified theories is based on their relevance to informing a model for the evaluation of ethical aspects of philanthropic strategies of charitable organizations.

As earlier stated, values of the social work profession are, of course, deontological in nature, but social workers sometimes use teleological consequential arguments, especially the utilitarian strand, to decide complex ethical dilemmas.[31] According to Elaine Congress and Frederic Reamer, most social workers do not even use a philosophical approach at all but base their decisions on other models of practical wisdom and moral reasoning when faced with ethical dilemmas, which is akin to phronesis as discussed in ethical perspectives from practical theology.[32]

In view of the foregoing, the ethical evaluation of philanthropic strategies of charitable organizations will be based on relevant ethical theoretical perspectives and the empirical research findings. In particular, Emmanuel

---

29. Richardson and Fowers, "Interpretive Social Science," 1, 17.

30. Osmer, *Practical Theology*, 77.

31. Opatrný, "Caritas Theory," 306–7; Šrajer, "Etika a Požadavek," 81–88; Kaptein and Wempe, "Three General Theories," 28.

32. Congress, "What Social Workers Should Know," 10; Reamer, "Ethical Theories," 20.

Kant's moral theory and the Ubuntu African traditional philosophy will be employed.

## Immanuel Kant's Moral Theory: The Categorical Imperative Procedure

In discussing the Kantian approach to ethics in philanthropy, Thomas Hill and Bojana Radovanović make several valuable contributions in addition to highlighting familiar features of the Kantian approach.[33] In his article entitled, "Kant's Moral Theory as a Guide in Philanthropy," Radovanović endeavors to sketch a guidance in philanthropy based on Kant's moral theory and argues that, under the framework of Kant's theory, we are morally obliged to relieve the sufferings and improve the happiness of others.[34] In support of this premise, Alice Walla further writes that

> Latitude creates the required space for the satisfaction of the agent's most important needs compatible with a genuine commitment to the promotion of the happiness of others, what Kant calls one's true needs.[35]

Kant defines philanthropy as love of human beings, which is a practical love, resulting in beneficence.[36] It is our duty to be beneficent and sacrificing a part of our welfare for the welfare of others. This is akin to the concept of charity as discussed in the second chapter of this book and, as it were, it underpins the praxis of Diakonia in Protestant theology, Caritas in Catholic theology, and Ubuntu in African traditional philosophy.

Thomas Hill notes that a proper application of Kantian moral theory to questions about philanthropy requires thinking about "midlevel moral principles for *imperfect* (non-ideal) moral agents in an *actual* and dangerously imperfect world."[37] In the same vein, he adds that this implies that the principles that we accept "should not be framed in utter disregard of the probability that in fact not everyone will do their fair share." Accordingly, a proper Kantian account of our obligations of beneficence might turn out to

---

33. Hill, "Duties and Choices," 13–39; Radovanović, "Kant's Moral Theory," 585–600.
34. Radovanović, "Kant's Moral Theory," 598.
35. Walla, "Kant's Moral Theory," 740.
36. Cf. Radovanović, "Kant's Moral Theory," 598.
37. Hill, "Duties and Choices," 20.

be more demanding than views according to which we are obligated only to do our fair part.

Kantian ethics are at the very base of the deontological ethical theory ascribed to the German philosopher Immanuel Kant.[38] Accordingly, this theory, which developed as a result of the Enlightenment rationalism, is based on the view that the only intrinsically good thing is a good will, implying that an action can only be good if its maxim—the principle behind it—is duty to the moral law. According to the African scholars Obinna Obiagwu and Jude Onuoha and other Kantian proponents, Kantian ethics are based on the moral theory that says people owe moral duties that are based on universal rules.[39] Other scholars further elaborate that Kantian ethics are a set of universal moral principles that apply to all human beings, regardless of context or situation.[40] Immanuel Kant calls these principles *Categorical Imperatives* and they are defined by their morality and level of freedom.[41] Accordingly, there is also a premise that people can use reasoning to reach ethical decisions. This reasoning allows social workers to act according to universally acceptable ethical principles such as others may act toward them and will make decisions based on positive outcomes.

This book builds on the premise that even if there were no policy to govern NGOs in a country such as was the case with Zambia, it is still imperative to evaluate the ethical aspects of philanthropic strategies employed by charitable organizations through ethical reflection on universally binding ethical principles. According to Richard Osmer, this will allow the respective organizations and moral communities to test their practices and norms against universally acceptable ethical standards.[42] As such, this theoretical perspective finds relevance for application in the scope of this book, namely ethics in philanthropy.

## The Categorical Imperative Procedure

Central to Kant's moral theory is the use of the categorical imperative procedure, which involves the testing of maxims for universalizability in order

---

38. Gomez, *Introduction to Ethics*, 262–63; Sandle, "What Is Kantian Ethics?"
39. Obiagwu and Onuoha, "Implication of Kant's Moral Philosophy," 30–32.
40. Schmidt, "Kantian Ethics."
41. Hill, *Blackwell Guide to Kant's Ethics*, 231.
42. Osmer, *Practical Theology*, 49.

to decide what to do, or even to construct all ethical truth.[43] In arguing for his formulation, Kant provisionally assumes that there are such things as basic moral principles and points out that the only thing that could count as a moral principle or "supreme practical principle" is a *categorical Imperative*, or a "universal practical law" that unconditionally demands compliance from everyone.[44] In support of Kant, Bojana Radovanović writes:

> When we consider whether an act that we want to undertake is morally right or wrong, we should test our principle of action, our maxim, against the categorical imperative.[45]

Kant formulates three versions of the categorical imperative, based on the principles of consistency, human dignity, and universality.[46] In doing so, he makes use of the concept of a "maxim", which is a principle on which one acts, and takes the form such as, "In such circumstances, do that." The maxim may or may not be a moral principle, but preferably and morally it should recommend a model course of action such as, *"If asked for my expenses, I ought to be truthful."*[47]

Since moral beliefs are universally binding, one key characteristic of holding a moral belief is consistency. Hence Kant's formula of universal law:

i. *Act only according to that maxim by which you can at the same time will that it should become a universal law.*

According to this formulation, Kant acknowledges the universal nature of morality.[48] In acknowledging that a person should be honest, he implies that the person ought to be consistent, and that others ought to do likewise in similar circumstances.[49] Likewise, by saying that one ought to be truthful, he implies that the person should do this whenever the same circumstances arise and that everyone should do so as well.

Kant's second formulation of the categorical imperative is:

---

43. Gomez, *Introduction to Ethics*, 262; Hill, *Blackwell Guide to Kant's Ethics*, 231; Kaptein and Wempe, "Three General Theories," 14.
44. Hill, *Blackwell Guide to Kant's Ethics*, 90.
45. Radovanović, "Kant's Moral Theory," 589.
46. BA Theories, "Kant's Ethical Theory."
47. BA Theories, "Kant's Ethical Theory."
48. Hill, *Blackwell Guide to Kant's Ethics*, 4.
49. BA Theories, "Kant's Ethical Theory."

ii.  *Act so that you treat humanity, whether in your own person or in that of another always as an end and never as a means only.*

This formulation is often referred to as the principle of "respect for persons" and is akin to the dignity and worth of the human person.[50] According to the just cited source (as per footnote) as well as Muel Kaptein and Johan Wempe, Kant is hereby acknowledging that moral judgements are not hypothetical, and that human beings are ends in themselves, not means to an end.[51] By illustration, it implies that if a human being is treated as a means to an end by another human being, that action is not a moral one. Barbara Herman writes, "In so far as one has ends at all, one has already willed the continued exercise of one's agency as a rational being."[52] According to Herman's later publication, these ends "come from what Kant calls the 'true needs' of human agents" and have to be met "if an agent is to function or continue to function as a rational, end-setting agent."[53] Furthermore, in accordance with Martin Sticker, true needs represent human priorities and the affected people themselves should determine their own needs and priorities.[54]

As such, Kant's formulation of humanity as an end requires that humans are never treated merely as means to an end, but always also as ends in themselves.[55]

In his third formulation of the categorical imperative Kant writes that:

iii.  *Act only so that the will through its maxims could regard itself at the same time as universally lawgiving.*

This is the principle of universality, or universalizability.[56] Accordingly, Kant is acknowledging here that it is not just one person who makes moral judgements, but everyone else is involved. Everyone is a lawgiver in this sense, and hence each one should reflect on whether it would be acceptable if everyone acted on the same maxim as her or him. This third formulation

---

50. BA Theories, "Kant's Ethical Theory."
51. Kaptein and Wempe, "Three General Theories," 16.
52. Herman, "Mutual Aid," 586.
53. Herman, "Murder and Mayhem," 424.
54. Sticker, "True Need in Kant," 432.
55. BA Theories, "Kant's Ethical Theory."
56. BA Theories, "Kant's Ethical Theory."

calls upon one to ask whether she or he would be willing for her or his action to be universalized.

## Summary of Kant's Moral Theory

In summary, Kant endeavours to base his moral theory on the principle of reason, in contrast to the utilitarians, who emphasized feelings. Accordingly, Kant uses reason to determine the nature of morality, and by so doing he holds that we can also ascertain the content of moral judgements, namely that one should only do what is universalizable, that one should respect persons, and that one should recognize that everyone is subject to the moral law.

In view of the foregoing, the Kantian moral theory is directly applicable to the main purpose of this book, namely, to evaluate the ethical aspects of philanthropic strategies of charitable organizations by testing the respective philanthropic strategies against universally acceptable ethical principles. The three formulations of the categorical imperatives are thus directly applicable, namely:

i. *Act only according to that maxim by which you can at the same time will that it should become a universal law.*

ii. *Act so that you treat humanity, whether in your own person or in that of another always as an end and never as a means only.*

iii. *Act only so that the will through its maxims could regard itself at the same time as universally lawgiving.*

The other theory employed along with Kant's moral theory is the Ubuntu African traditional philosophy as discussed hereafter.

## African "Ubuntu" Philosophy

Social work is a function of and response to many different contexts in which it operates.[57] According to Believe Okwokwo and Michal Opatrný, social work involves understanding and addressing various social, cultural, economic, and political factors that impact individuals, families, and communities in their various and respective contexts.[58] As such, the evaluation

---

57. Ife, "Realising the Purpose," 2.
58. Okwokwo, "Social Work in a Global Context"; Opatrný, "Caritas Theory," 303.

of ethical aspects of philanthropic strategies of charitable organizations operating among poor African communities should also take into consideration the traditional cultural practices and belief systems of the local people. In this case and as the Zimbabwean scholar Vincent Mabvurira also writes, ethical issues in social work practice with people of African descent should also be guided by African Ubuntu philosophy.[59]

"Ubuntu" is one of the core and probably most significant principles of traditional African culture.[60] According to Mabvurira, Ubuntu refers to a collection of values and practices that black people of Africa or of African origin view as making people authentic human beings.[61] Even though the nuances of these values and practices vary across different ethnic groups, they all point to one thing, namely, that an authentic individual human being is part of a larger and more significant relational, communal, societal, environmental, and spiritual world. Ubuntu is a philosophy, a spirituality, and an ethic of African traditional life.[62] Therefore, an evaluation of ethical aspects of philanthropic strategies of charities in an African context such as Zambia should also be framed within a narrative that appeals to the contextual conceptualization of such ethics as Ubuntu. An excerpt from an article that once appeared in the Zambian public media (*Lusaka Times*) on May 8, 2016, succinctly sums up the conceptualization and practice of Ubuntu among Zambians as follows:

> Africa oh Africa. Africa our motherland; the land of natural beauty and unity. Where everything belonged to everyone and children to the community, all in the spirit of Ubuntu. "Ubuntu"—an African Bantu word, is a philosophy that reflects the human in us. It gives an understanding of who we are as human beings and how we relate to the rest of the universe. Humanity, unity, compassion, love, peace, and harmony in the African culture are everything that makes this continent so unique. As South Africa's Archbishop Desmond Tutu passionately speaks of Ubuntu, "My humanity is caught up, is inextricably bound up, in yours. We belong in a bundle of life. We say, 'A person is a person through other persons.'"[63]

---

59. Mabvurira, "Hunhu/Ubuntu Philosophy," 74.
60. Wet, *Understanding Transformational Development*, 28.
61. Mabvurira, "Hunhu/Ubuntu Philosophy," 74.
62. Carneades.org, "What is Ubuntu Philosophy?"; Metz, "African Ethic of Ubuntu."
63. Jovago, "Whatever Happened to the Spirit of Ubuntu?"

In the autobiographical book of his *Long Walk to Freedom*, Nelson Mandela, one of the great moral and political leaders of our time and former president of South Africa, writes:

> I have always known that deep down in every human heart, there is mercy and generosity. No one is born hating another person because of the color of his skin, or his background, or his religion. People must learn to hate, and if they can learn to hate, they can be taught to love, for love comes more naturally to the human heart than the opposite.[64]

Although the word "Ubuntu" does not appear in this excerpt, it is still undisputable that Mandela is writing from an Ubuntu background because it was his philosophy and motivation too as Claire Oppenheim also reckons.[65]

In an article entitled, "Hunhu/Ubuntu Philosophy as a Guide for Ethical Decision Making in Social Work," the Zimbabwean author, Vincent Mabvurira writes that one of the supreme contributions of the peoples of Africa to the worldview is the Ubuntu philosophy.[66] The word "Ubuntu" is derived from a commonality or similarity of Bantu languages of Africa, and it is, therefore, an African philosophy. For instance, among the Lozi people of Western Zambia, the word for human being is "mutu" and Ubuntu is "Butu," and it means exactly the same as Ubuntu in all other Zambian languages such as Bemba (Ubuntu), Tonga (Buntu), and Nyanja (Umuntu). As earlier mentioned, Ubuntu is a core principle of traditional African culture, and it implies humanness—the condition and quality of being human.[67] As Johann Broodryk writes, Ubuntu is based on the values of humanness, caring, respect, compassion, and associated values that ensure a happy and qualitative human life in a communal and family spirit.[68]

From the foregoing discourse, it is quite vivid that the values of Ubuntu are akin to deontological ethics in charity. As such, they can also be employed to evaluate ethics in philanthropy in accordance with the scope of this book.

Apparently, the African traditional worldview of Ubuntu seems to have no direct equivalent in Western philosophical thought,[69] but it does,

64. Mandela, *Long Walk to Freedom*, 542.
65. Oppenheim, "Nelson Mandela," 371.
66. Mabvurira, "Hunhu/Ubuntu Philosophy," 74.
67. Wet, *Understanding Transformational Development*, 28.
68. Broodryk, *Ubuntu* [2004], 31.
69. Kgatla, "Relationships Are Building Blocks."

nevertheless, complement the Western social thought in many respects. Nkonko Kamwangamalu, an outstanding professor of English and linguistics at Howard University, describes Ubuntu as a community-based mindset in which the welfare of the group is greater than the welfare of a single individual member of the group, something similar to the sum total of synergy.[70] Individuality, that is the sense of self, is, however, recognized as important in the concept of Ubuntu, as opposed to individualism that seeks to promote selfish interests at the expense of common good.[71] Individualism is, therefore, not acceptable in the Ubuntu sense of morality. To the contrary, Ubuntu revolves around universally acceptable ethical values such as justice and fairness.[72]

It must be underscored that Ubuntu is also different from many common religious and spiritual concepts such as faith, grace, or the divine, which are essentially descriptive of a state of being, rather than having a prescriptive moral meaning that refers explicitly to the moral directive to create community.[73] Accordingly, a person can have more or less ubuntu in proportion to his conduct towards his fellow humans, thereby making himself more or less of a genuine human being. As Andrea Ng'weshemi writes, "For Africans, one is not human simply by birth. Rather one becomes human through a progressive process of integration into society."[74] Therefore, the drive of Ubuntu spirit is to become fully and genuinely human, in unity with fellow humans.[75] The active nature of Ubuntu does not limit it to a static state, and the ability to gain ubuntu lies at the center of every African. By implication, if all human individuals contain within themselves a common core of decency as described by Nelson Mandela, then every individual must also have the ability to access this core value and, if their heart is touched, they are capable of changing.[76] This core of decency and humanity is also a core value of Ubuntu itself. Ethically, this core value enables a human being to act according to the good will as held by Kantian ethics too.

---

70. Kamwangamalu, "Ubuntu in South Africa," 24–42.
71. Broodryk, *Ubuntu* [2002], 42.
72. Mabvurira, "Hunhu/Ubuntu Philosophy," 74.
73. Oppenheim, "Nelson Mandela," 371.
74. Ng'weshemi, *Rediscovering the Human*, 15.
75. Oppenheim, "Nelson Mandela," 371.
76. Mandela, *Long Walk to Freedom*, 462.

Furthermore, communalism and communitarian morality, unlike communism, are also core values of Ubuntu and imply that although the interests of the individual are subordinate to those of the group, the community should also focus on the interests of the individual members and those activities and behaviors that will ensure the good of the group.[77] Ubuntu is, therefore, a collective solidarity, meaning that individuals will align their interests, activities, and loyalties to the group's cause and wellbeing.[78] According to Desmond Tutu, a South African borne iconic Pan Africanist and Nobel Peace Prize winner, Ubuntu speaks about wholeness and compassion.[79] Tutu further argues that a person with ubuntu (humanness) is welcoming, hospitable, warm, generous, and willing to share, a conceptualization that is very much akin to philanthropy from a deontological ethical perspective.

In view of the foregoing discourse, it can be deduced that Ubuntu stands for communitarian morality. As African Congolese scholar Mbangu Muyingi writes, the goal of this morality is dignity, reached through personal growth and fulfilment.[80] Accordingly, the participation of the community is the essential means to personal dignity and hence this participation is the motive and fulfilment of the process of morality. As such, everything that promotes personal dignity and participation in the community is good, whereas everything that prevents these values is bad. Said another way, the moral possibility of Ubuntu intrinsically relates to human happiness and fulfilment within a community. According John Mbiti, one of Africa's contemporary eminent philosophers and Christian theologians of Kenyan origin, this means the demand to participate in community, yet not only for the sake of personal fulfilment but also for the sake of the fulfilment of the whole community, because only in the community is personal fulfilment thought possible.[81]

Another key aspect worthy highlighting is that the Ubuntu attitude towards others is to treat the other as self, which is akin to the golden rule (do to others as you would like them to do to you) and the greatest commandment (love your neighbour as yourself).[82] As stated in the discussion

---

77. See Broodryk, *Ubuntu* [2002], 42; Muyingi, "African Ethics," 564.
78. Mogkoro, "Ubuntu and the Law," 45.
79. Tutu, *God Has a Dream*.
80. Muyingi, "African Ethics," 564–65.
81. Mbiti, *African Religions and Philosophy*, 223–56.
82. Shutte, *Ubuntu*, 31.

on Kantian ethics and foregoing excerpts in this section, Ubuntu is also underpinned by the concept of love such as is taught by Christianity. Consequently, and like any other moral ideology, Ubuntu provides rules or normative ethics such as corporate governance and guides Africans to live good lives daily.[83]

Suffice it to state at this stage that the concept of Ubuntu is key to understanding Africa traditional ethics as Mbangu Muyingi also observes.[84] Accordingly, whenever a person does not respect the life and dignity of other persons, she or he automatically loses her or his humanity because humanity is thought to be the essence of being human. Muyingi clearly states that it is the notion of humanity that constitutes the foundation of all traditional African ethics. According to Wim van Binsbergen, Ubuntu recognizes four attributes of being human, which are essentially ethics, and these are: human dignity, equality, universal brotherhood and sisterhood, and sacredness of life.[85] These attributes provide the most desirable state of life in community-based living. Consequently, any conduct that does not respect the dignity of human life is bad, and whatever contributes to the protection and the intensification of human life is good. Hence Ndungi Mungai emphasizes that whatever is good for humanity is Ubuntu and whatever harms humanity is against Ubuntu.[86] Now, this is a very critical ethical premise with regard to the ethical evaluation of philanthropic strategies employed by charitable organizations operating around Africa.

## *Summary of Ubuntu Ethics Relevant for Evaluation of Philanthropic Strategies*

In summary, the overarching Ubuntu ethic is being human with humanness. Regarding the topic under discussion in this book, it means charitable organizations ought to have the acceptable qualities of humanness in the execution of their philanthropic strategies. As Vincent Mabvurira writes, the other ethics are as, but not limited to the following:

i. Consider the good of the majority or community over personal good (communitarian morality).

---

83. Muyingi, "African Ethics," 565.
84. Muyingi, "African Ethics," 561–62.
85. Binsbergen, *Reconciliation*, 19.
86. Mungai, "Afrocentric Social Work," 74.

ii. The course of action chosen (philanthropic strategy) should treat individuals equally (social justice/fairness).

iii. Respect, love, care, and compassion for others, especially the vulnerable (dignity and worth of the human person / social justice).

iv. Should bring no harm or pain to all the parties involved (no harm or pain).[87]

Moving forward, the ethical evaluation of philanthropic strategies of charitable organizations as revealed by the empirical research findings will be based on the foregoing Ubuntu ethics, along with Kant's categorical imperative ethical procedure.

## Evaluation of Ethical Aspects of Philanthropic Strategies

When the ethical aspects of philanthropic strategies implicit in the empirical research findings are evaluated against the relevant ethical theories discussed in the previous section, several ethical violations inherent in the philanthropic strategies of charitable organizations are unearthed as hereafter stated and explained.

### Lack of Ethic of Love

Ethical philanthropy flows out of love for humanity. As per Kantian ethics, philanthropy is defined as love of human beings, which is a practical love, resulting in beneficence.[88] According to the just cited author with reference to the footnote, it is our duty to be beneficent by sacrificing part of our welfare for others. This is akin to the concept of charity discussed in chapter 2 and as already stated, it underpins the praxis of Diakonia in Protestant theology, Caritas in Catholic theology, and Ubuntu in African traditional philosophy.

Apparently, the empirical research revealed several unethical aspects that point to the lack of an ethic of love in the philanthropic strategies of charitable organizations that operated in Mongu town and the country of Zambia at large, such as lack of respect for persons, unequal regard, and tribalism. Said another way, these unethical practices and several others

---

87. Mabvurira, "Hunhu/Ubuntu Philosophy," 75.
88. Radovanović, "Kant's Moral Theory," 598.

as contained in the research results are as a result of the lack of an ethic of love, because true beneficence flows out of love according to Kantian ethics.

In understanding these unethical vices, it is imperative to recapitulate that philanthropy evolves from the biblical concept of love.[89] As Osmer writes, Christian love should be understood and expressed as an ethic of equal regard because human beings are created in the image of God and are, therefore, worthy of respect in personal relationships and fair treatment in social institutions.[90] In the narratives of Christ's ministry, he (Christ) is portrayed as telling his disciples at least eight times that they ought to love their neighbours as themselves (the Greatest Commandment) and follow the golden rule—do to others what you would like them to do to you. Osmer also states that general principles such as love can help us to understand and address moral issues at stake in episodes, situations, and contexts, which in this case entail ethics in philanthropy.[91] As it were, it is undisputable that both the Greatest Commandment and Golden Rule as taught in biblical and pastoral theology were being violated by the philanthropic strategies of charitable organizations in the communities of Mongu and evidently in Zambia as a country.

Equally, the Ubuntu attitude towards others is to treat the other as self, which is also like the golden rule and the greatest commandment.[92] As stated in the discussion on Kantian ethics, Ubuntu is also underpinned by the concept of love such as taught in Christian theology. Consequently, and like any other moral ideology, it provides moral rules or normative ethics, and guides Africans to live good and ethical lives daily.[93] As it were, some of the core ethics of Ubuntu are "respect, love, care, and compassion for others, especially the vulnerable."[94] As such, a violation of love for fellow humans is also a violation of the African Ubuntu philosophy, just as it is against the Kantian ethics of moral law, too.

An observation is hereby made that the lack of an ethic of love in the philanthropic strategies of charitable organizations can also be perceived as the root of all other ethical violations as revealed by the subsequent ethical evaluations hereafter.

89. Garcia-Irons, *Place of Spirituality*, 1–7.
90. Osmer, *Practical Theology*, 151.
91. Osmer, *Practical Theology*, 152.
92. Shutte, *Ubuntu*, 31.
93. Muyingi, "African Ethics," 565.
94. Mabvurira, "Hunhu/Ubuntu Philosophy," 75.

## Using Humans as Means Only

One of the serious ethical violations pertaining to philanthropic strategies by charities such as operated in Mongu district of Western Zambia was using people as means rather than ends in themselves, and that could be summed up one respondent's recapitulated response: "They are just using us to enrich themselves. Nothing is happening!" That was evidenced by the fact that there were no convincing tangible results seen from the work of charities despite their presence in the area from precolonial times.[95] According to Kant's principle of respect of persons, one should "act so that you treat humanity, whether in your own person or in that of another always as an end and never as a means only." Therefore, this praxis of just using people by the said charitable organizations cannot be accepted as a universal maxim according to the rest of the Kantian ethics.

Such inhuman attitude towards other humans is also totally against the most basic African traditional ethics embraced by Ubuntu philosophy, which, *inter alia*, requires one to consider the good of the majority as well when thinking of personal good. Ubuntu stands for communitarian morality and the goal of that morality is human dignity, reached through personal growth and fulfilment.[96] Accordingly, participation of the community is the motive and fulfilment of the process of morality.

On the contrary, the empirical research revealed that most of the local people did not participate in either the formulation or execution of philanthropic strategies of charitable NGOs that operated in their communities. Consequently, they did not even know about the operational strategies of the respective NGOs. The most noticeable aspect to the participants was that the livelihoods of the officials of NGOs improved drastically. The following excerpt from a respondent is a good sample statement in this regard:

> So, whereas the economy of the people looks the same or deteriorates, the personal economies of the heads of those NGOs seem to improve. That's what brings a bad name on the NGOs. They don't seem to deliver!

In view of both Kantian universalizable ethics and African Ubuntu philosophy, using fellow humans as means, and worse so to selfish ends, is a serious ethical violation.

---

95. MCDSS, *NGO File 2018*, 1–2.
96. Muyingi, "African Ethics," 564–65.

## Showing the Workings

### Unequal Treatment of Clients / Unequal Distribution of Resources

Ubuntu ethics require that the course of action chosen should treat individuals equally. According to Vincent Mabvurira, this means treating individuals with respect, love, care, and compassion, especially the vulnerable members of society.[97] To the contrary, the empirical research into ethical aspects of philanthropic strategies of NGOs in Mongu revealed that there were issues of greed and interest for personal gain, corruption, and vulnerable members of the community being overlooked in the process. Furthermore, most NGOs concentrated on urban areas at the expense of the people in rural areas, making it difficulties for the most and truly vulnerable members of society to access their services. All these aspects are recipes for unequal distribution of resources and unequal treatment of clients as evidenced in the research.

When evaluated against Kant's threefold formula of universal law, neither unequal treatment of clients nor unequal distribution of resources pass the test and neither of them can be universalised, rendering both of them unethical.

### Not Addressing True Needs of the People

Human ends are directly connected to true needs of the respective people.[98] The previous section has made a clear discourse that humans should never be treated as means only, but ever as ends. In the empirical research findings, the participants, who were mainly local people and government officials, expressed their real pressing problems and felt needs, which are referred to as *"true needs"* in Kantian ethics.[99] On the other hand, the participants who were mainly top officials of NGOs described the philanthropic strategies employed by charitable organizations, most of which apparently did not address the true needs of the people that they claimed to help, rendering such interventions unethical.

According to the African Ubuntu philosophical ethics, the charitable organizations should "consider the good of the majority community over personal good."[100] This also directly implies that the identified needs should

---

97. Mabvurira, "Hunhu/Ubuntu Philosophy," 75.
98. Herman, "Murder and Mayhem," 424.
99. Sticker, "True Need in Kant," 432–34.
100. Mabvurira, "Hunhu/Ubuntu Philosophy," 75.

serve not just the interest of some privileged individuals, but that of the community at large according to the prioritization of needs by the local people themselves, which is an equivalent dynamic of true needs. As it were, the moral possibility of Ubuntu intrinsically relates to human happiness and fulfilment within a community. As John Mbiti writes, this means the demand to participate in community, yet not only for the sake of personal fulfilment but also for the sake of the fulfilment of the whole community, because only in the community is personal fulfilment thought possible.[101]

In view of the foregoing, the philanthropic strategies of charities in Mongu and Zambia at large were found to be unethical because they did not address true needs of the local people. Ethical philanthropy must address true needs of the people.

*Untruthfulness*

In Kantian ethics, "truth is conformity of the cognition to the object in concreto."[102] By implication, there must be concrete agreement of what something appears to be and its essence, that is, what it really is.[103] As earlier illustrated, "If asked for my expenses, I ought to be truthful."[104] Apparently, it can be argued right from the problematic issue that triggered the research for this book that some, if not most of the information reported by the charities was either insufficient or misrepresentative of the truth that was required for effective monitoring and regulation of the respective charities.[105] The empirical research verified this theoretical discovery as participants expected the NGOs to be practical and true as per the following sample excerpt from one participant:

> That is why we're saying we need those NGOs to do what they say. If they say we need our organization to take care of orphans, let them take care of the orphans. If they say we need our organization to take care of old aged people, let them do so, let them do that. So, in several cases we've seen they say this and what is happening is different.

---

101. Mbiti, *African Religions and Philosophy*, 223–56.
102. Kant, *Prolegomena*, 26.
103. Sher, "Lessons on Truth from Kant," 184.
104. BA Theories, "Kant's Ethical Theory."
105. Hasnan et al., *Issues, Challenges*, 777.

There is no agreement between the cognition and the object to the extent that some, if not most of the NGOs were not even visible to the community according to the following citation of one participant: "You can have these organizations, but when you look at their visibility they're just existing on papers. So, that has also contributed to, you know, few organizations that are providing charity work."

Truthfulness as a moral value is also inherent in the African Ubuntu philosophy, wherein the goal of morality is dignity that is reached through personal growth and fulfilment in a spirit of communalism and family.[106] In Vincent Mabvurira's view, the moral value of truthfulness in Ubuntu also entails social justice such as the community deserving to know the truth about the charitable organizations that operate in their area.[107] As such, untruthfulness is unethical even from the perspective of Ubuntu because it is not good for communitarian morality and humanity in general. Just like it cannot be universalized under Kantian ethics, Ndungi Mungai also writes that "whatever is good for humanity is Ubuntu and whatever harms humanity is against Ubuntu."[108] This is a serious discrepancy in terms of the ethicality of the philanthropic strategies employed by charitable organizations as it compromises critical desired ethical standards such as transparency and accountability, proper monitoring and evaluation, and ultimately undermines human dignity and value in both the individual and community.

*Harmful Practices to Community*

One of the core values of the African Ubuntu philosophy is to cause *no harm or pain* to all parties involved.[109] This is also directly related to one of the core ethical considerations of the work of this book, wherein respect "refers to the avoidance of social and personal harm" to participants, who in this case are also the recipients of charitable goods and services from charitable organizations.[110]

Apparently, most of the reasons for failure by charitable NGOs to make impact as cited in the Mongu case can be categorized as being rather

106. Muyingi, "African Ethics," 564.
107. Mabvurira, "Hunhu/Ubuntu Philosophy," 74–75.
108. Mungai, "Afrocentric Social Work," 74.
109. Mabvurira, "Hunhu/Ubuntu Philosophy," 75.
110. Hugman, "Social Work Research," 152.

harmful practices to the desired communitarian morality as embraced by Ubuntu. For example, tribalism, corruption, indigenous people not supportive to development initiatives in their homeland, interest for personal gain and misappropriation of resources, etc., are all harmful to the community because they, among others, erode social justice, respect for diversity, equality and fairness, and practical moral reasoning that is necessary for ethical decision-making in philanthropic and all other forms social work. If unchecked, these vices can breed internal conflict, which is development in reverse as it reduces economic growth by about 2.3 percent per year on national scale according to research.[111] Therefore, such practices as cited herein are deemed harmful to the communitarian life because they are divisive and cause pain, suffering, and conflict within, rather than uniting and bringing happiness and economic growth and transformation to the community.

When evaluated against Kant's moral theory, the reasons why charitable organizations failed to bring about positive change in Mongu cannot be universalized or accepted as universal moral standards. For instance, it is unethical for one to will that selfishness or interest for personal gain be made universal law or everybody acts selfishly. The litmus test here is the categorical imperative, as supported by Bojana Radovanović, that "when we consider whether an act that we want to undertake is morally right or wrong, we should test our principle of action, our maxim, against the categorical imperative."[112]

It is commonplace to rationalize that harmful practices such as inherent in the charitable organizations such as operated in Mongu and Zambia cannot bring about any positive change. This explains why some, if not most charities have not made positive impact so far.

## Summary Perspectives on Showing the Workings

The research results have been thoroughly discussed in this chapter and all participants were selected purposefully, being local resident for at least five years, NGO officials, and government officials in oversight institutions . I also had to adhere to gender representativeness as well as inclusion of young people in the research interviews. Furthermore, the research followed a multi-method approach (interviews, field notes, observations, and

---

111. Collier, *Bottom Billion*, 27.
112. Radovanović, "Kant's Moral Theory," 589.

triangulation) in order to come up with a rich and meaningful description of the philanthropic strategies employed by charitable organizations that operated in the area. The respondents expressed dissatisfaction at the philanthropic strategies employed by charitable organizations that operated in their communities and there was need to review the ethicality of the praxis of the said charities.

Two relevant theories have been employed to evaluate the ethicality of the research results with regard to the philanthropic strategies employed by charitable organizations, namely, Kant's moral theory and African traditional philosophy of Ubuntu. The evaluation of the research results against the two ethical theories revealed ethical violations such as, but not limited to, lack of an ethic of love, using people as means instead of as ends in themselves, not addressing true needs of the people, unequal treatment of clients, untruthfulness, and practices that were harmful to the community. There is, therefore, need for an ethical review of the philanthropic strategies by charitable organizations such as operated in Mongu district and all of Zambia, as well as other African communities from time to time.

The next chapter will focus on establishing action-guiding concepts aimed at developing a new praxis and model that will guide the evaluation of ethical aspects of philanthropic strategies of charitable organizations, both in the local and wider contexts of society.

# 6

# Model for Ethical Evaluation of Philanthropic Strategies

## INTRODUCTION

This chapter forms the most abstract and flagship part of the scope of this book as major concepts from the preceding chapters that, of course, represent specific research tasks are synchronized and transformed into high-level insights and action-guiding concepts so that a new praxis and model for evaluating ethical aspects of philanthropic strategies by charitable organizations is formulated. In this chapter, discussions of empirical research findings are connected with theoretical perspectives in the broader spectrum in order to promote evidence-informed practice with theory-informed practice as Michael Austin writes.[1] Malcolm Payne also writes that there is need to bridge the perceived gap between practice and theory in academic research, where theory is often viewed as some speculation that is separate from practice.[2] As such, I hereby postulate that theory in social work does not only inform practice but is also developed from practice and is, therefore, also evidence-informed . In view of the foregoing, this chapter focuses on developing a model for evaluating ethical aspects of philanthropic strategies employed by charitable organizations, based on both empirical and theoretical discourses so far explored.

Without demeaning the supremacy of empirical evidence in any way, other data from all the preceding research tasks are hereby considered and

1. Austin, "Identifying the Conceptual Foundations," 15–31.
2. Payne, *Modern Social Work Theory*, 4.

treated with equal regard in order to develop a new praxis that responds to both practical and theoretical dimensions of the research problem and question. According to my earlier doctoral research on a practical theological model for a community transformation strategy, the resultant new praxis must be able to inform a holistic approach to the evaluation of ethics in philanthropic strategies employed by charitable organizations.[3]

As such, brief reflections on the perspectives from the preceding chapters of this book are presented and accompanied by the respective action-guiding concepts. This will be followed by specific concepts resulting from a synthesis of the detailed discourses of the preceding tasks. I thereafter propose and present a model for evaluating philanthropic strategies of charitable organizations from an interdisciplinary perspective comprising practical theology, social work, and common law.

The hermeneutical interaction among the preceding chapters and perspectives presented in this book is hereby regarded as an important aspect that also gives this chapter its unique place in the scope of the book.[4] As it were, empirical research gathers and analyses data that help to discern patterns and dynamics in particular episodes, situations, or contexts, while theoretical research draws on theories of the arts and sciences to better understand and explain why the patterns and dynamics are occurring. The practical task then is to determine strategies of action that will influence situations in ways that are desirable and enter into reflective conversation with the talk back emerging when the strategies are implemented. As such, the research tasks interrelate in such a way that issues emerging in one task may open new insights or necessitate further probe in another task.[5]

## SUMMARY OF PERSPECTIVES FROM PRECEDING TASKS

First, summaries of the perspectives identified from the preceding research tasks as contained in the preceding chapters of this book will be provided, followed by a unification of these concepts into themes and sub-themes. This will be followed by a reflection of how the concepts between the various phases interact with each other, in order to establish a framework for the development of action-guiding concepts that will lead to a new praxis and formulation of a practicable model for evaluating ethical aspects of

3. Mutemwa, "Practical Theological Model," 28.
4. Osmer, *Practical Theology*, 4–11.
5. Osmer, *Practical Theology*, 10.

philanthropic strategies employed by charitable organizations. The relationships amongst concepts is established with the help of James Dickoff et al.'s tested survey list of seven questions.[6]

## Summary of Theoretical Perspectives

A summary of theoretical perspectives is hereby provided and these contain related key ethical aspects, which then constitute action-guiding concepts that will inform a new praxis and model for the evaluation of ethical aspects of philanthropic strategies by charitable organizations.

### Guiding Purpose of the Study

The guiding purpose or aim of the study was to evaluate the ethical aspects of philanthropic strategies employed by charitable organizations operating in Mongu district of Zambia's Western Province, which was also as national and global issue that called for ethical reflection with universal principles.

### Ethical Reflection with Universal Ethical Principles

Even if there were no specific policy to govern NGOs in a country, it is still imperative to evaluate the ethical aspects of philanthropic strategies employed by charitable organizations through ethical reflection with universal ethical principles in order to allow the respective organizations and moral communities to test their practices and norms against universally acceptable ethical standards.[7]

### Theoretical Perspectives from Pastoral Theology

The concepts of "charity" and "charitable purpose" evolve from a theological background and can be located within the pastoral theological theory, which embraces applied theology in Catholic theology and practical theology in the Protestant theological discourse. The dialogue of pastoral theology is, however, not restricted to the Christian community and sources, but involves critical reflection on the church's dialogue with Christian sources

---

6. Dickoff et al., "Theory in a Practice Discipline," 434–35.
7. Osmer, *Practical Theology*, 49.

and other communities of experience and interpretation so as to guide the church's action toward holistic transformation. As such, it has been deductively inferred that the theoretical framework for the subject under study comprises pastoral theology, social work, and common law. Accordingly, the respective ethical perspectives from pastoral theology comprise ethical reflection with universal ethical principles, equal regard, good practice, and practical moral reasoning.

## *Theoretical Perspectives from Social Work*

Principles of social justice, human rights, collective responsibility, and respect for diversities underpin social work practice. Apparently, the discourse of social work is also enriched significantly by theological ethics through theology's criticism of the limited focus of professional ethics of social work, which focus mainly on deontological and utilitarian ethics.

Although the issue of ethics in social work is not easily reconciled globally, which is customary of social work discourse, it is generally accepted that ethics in social work can be summed into six fundamental foci. These are: social justice, service, dignity and worth of the human person, integrity, importance of human relationships, and competence. Apparently, these ethical categories or perspectives are directly applicable to the ethical evaluation of philanthropic strategies employed by charitable organizations.

Another area of ethical consideration from the perspective of social work concerns spirituality in social work as the origins of social work are in the practices of spirituality and religion and the principles thereof are based on the biblical idea of charity. The discrepancy between the rising concerns for more common use of spirituality in social work practice in the field and the lack of formal training and education in spirituality for social workers poses serious ethical implications for the field of social work. As such, the perspective of spirituality in social work has definite implications for the subject hereby under study.

Suffice it also to mention that ethical dilemmas arise when two or more ethical principles clash and this calls for ethical decision-making or practical moral reasoning.

## Theoretical Perspectives from Common Law

The ethical perspectives from common law regarding philanthropic strategies of charitable organizations are based on a threefold criterion of theoretical interpretation, ethical reflection, and good practice. Accordingly, theoretical interpretation of charity and charitable purposes should remind charities of their ethical obligations as they design their respective philanthropic strategies. Similarly, common law enforces that a charity must have a charitable purpose and be for the benefit of the public. The ethical question arising from theoretical interpretation of charity and charitable purpose is whether the philanthropic strategies of charitable organizations operating in poor African communities adhere to the dictates of common law pertaining to charities and charitable purposes?

Ethical reflection includes the aspects of equality and fairness, right to self-determination, deserving and undeserving poor, and transparency and accountability. Good practice applies directly to the aspect of common law concerning charities and charitable purposes as it involves deriving acceptable norms from exploring models of such practice in the present and past or by engaging reflexivity in transforming practice in the present. As it were, the aspects of theoretical interpretation and ethical reflection also constitute good practice with regard to the subject under investigation. For a better understanding, this has been presented in form of an equation recapitulated as follows:

Theoretical Interpretation + Ethical Reflection = Good Practice.

## Summary of Empirical Perspectives

A summary of the empirical perspectives is hereby provided with the related ethical aspects, which will also constitute action-guiding concepts to inform a new praxis and model for the evaluation of ethical aspects of philanthropic strategies by charitable organizations.

### Reasons for Failure by Charitable Organizations to Make Positive Impact

The empirical research overwhelmingly revealed that the charitable organizations operating in Mongu failed to make any positive impact in the community so far. Participants in the research cited several reasons for the failure, some of which were related to the *social and cultural* characteristics of the local people, while others were related to the *operational praxis* of the NGOs themselves. As it were, most of the reasons cited bordered on serious ethical issues such as social justice, equality and fairness, transparency and accountability, integrity, good practice, practical moral reasoning, respect for diversities, and ethical reflection with universal ethical principles in general. Other related aspects such as ethical dilemmas, sustainability and self-determination were also evident in the expectations of the participants.

In an interview, one of the participants lamented that NGOs were just exploiting people for their own benefits. Outrightly, the dignity and worth of the human person was being violated in that case! Several other participants expressed views that raised questions regarding the ethicality of the charitable organizations.

## True Needs

Key to implementation of effective philanthropic strategies is accurate understanding of real pressing problems and felt needs of the people, which are also referred to as true needs.[8] During the interviews, participants revealed that their true needs were *poverty, lack of employment and empowerment, transport and communication, education, health, and climate change.* Apparently, they also noted that philanthropic strategies of most NGOs in the area did not address their true needs, an aspect that bordered on serious ethical issues such as community participation in identifying and addressing their needs, giving for noble causes, as well as deserving and deserving poor. Other connected ethical aspects in this regard are social justice and again, ethical reflection with universal ethical principles.

## Philanthropic Strategies Employed by NGOs

Philanthropy is about addressing people's true needs. Two extremely opposing views were held regarding the strategies employed by charitable organizations in the local context of Mongu and, apparently, each respective view was held by an interested party. On one hand, participants from the local community and government expressed ignorance about the strategies employed by the said NGOs, with some at most indicating that the

---

8. Gautier, "Building a Philanthropic Strategy"; Sticker, "True Need in Kant," 432–34.

NOGs were biased and irrational in their strategies. On the other hand, officials of NGOs themselves mentioned a handful of techniques that they employed in executing their philanthropic strategies, namely networking with government and other stakeholders, community sensitisation, capacity building, and connecting with churches, under which there was also an appeal to spirituality as a strategy for success.

The big question, therefore, was whether those strategies actually addressed the real pressing problems and felt needs of the local people or not. An observation is hereby made that most of the strategies that the NGOs claimed to employ did not actually address the true needs of the local people as expressed in the previous section, except for capacity building, a scenario that is not in tandem with ethics in philanthropy if not qualified by other ethical aspects like sustainability, as well as transparency and accountability and ultimately, using humans as ends, not means. This is probably why the non-NGO participants expressed ignorance about the philanthropic strategies by the NGOs in their area. For instance, the empirical research also revealed that there were too many workshops conducted by NGOs that only benefited the facilitators in terms of allowances. Clearly, other ethical aspects such as good practice, ethical reflection with universal ethical principles, practical moral reasoning, as well as good practice were also at stake in this case.

*Expectations Regarding Charitable Organizations*

It is notable from the empirical research results that the people's expectations were connected to their own true needs. As it were, the goals of philanthropy in developing countries are to help communities rebuild, advance, become sustainable, and eliminate social and economic inequality.[9] As such, participants expected NGOs to bring about positive impact in the community.

Among others, participants expected NGOs to advocate for social justice, uplift the living standards of the people by empowering them and providing employment where possible, supplement government efforts, and to be well coordinated among themselves as NGOs to avoid unethical practices such as duplicity of philanthropic activities. Furthermore, the work of NGOs was expected to cover both rural and urban areas, be monitored and evaluated by independent members of the local communities,

9. Burgess-Van Aken, "Goals of Philanthropy."

help vulnerable members of the community, starting with the neediest, as well as to be practical and true to their word and course. The local people also expected the NGOs to be conducting community research to identify the true needs of the people before moving in with their philanthropic agendas, as well as building the capacity of the local people in such a way that philanthropic aid should not disempower them and cause dependency, but help them to be self-sustaining.

Finally, the study also identified some critical ethical aspects implicit in the expectations of the local people regarding the operations of charitable organizations. Again in no particular order, these include ethical reflection with universal ethical principles, social justice, integrity, good practice, deserving and undeserving poor, and transparency and accountability.

## SUMMARY OF ACTION-GUIDING CONCEPTS FOR EVALUATING ETHICAL ASPECTS OF PHILANTHROPIC STRATEGIES BY CHARITABLE ORGANIZATIONS

This section provides a summary of the major concepts for evaluating ethical aspects of philanthropic strategies of charitable organizations as emergent from critical pragmatic reflection of the preceding tasks of the work of this book. The identified major concepts are:

i. Ethical reflection,
ii. Community participation,
iii. Defining community true needs, and
iv. Philanthropic strategy.

Reference to detailed discussions of the presented concepts is hereby made to the respective previous chapters and sections from where they have been extracted. However, a summary of these concepts is hereby provided as a reflection on what has already been discussed in details in the previous chapters.

*Ethical reflection* in this case is supported by aspects such as reflection with universal ethical principles regarding charitable organizations, ethic of love, social justice, human rights, and collective responsibility. It also includes respect for diversity, equality and fairness, right to self-determination, as well as the aspect of deserving and undeserving poor. Furthermore, transparency and accountability as well as good practice equally form integral units of the concept of ethical reflection with universal principles.

The concept of *community participation* is buttressed by the promotion of citizen participation in strategy formulation and implementation, as well as sustainability of community social and development initiatives. This is also directly connected to the concept of *defining community true needs* that requires prior community research and understanding community expectations as they relate to the true needs of the people.

The fourth emergent major concept—*philanthropic strategy*—entails understanding the goals of philanthropy such as ethical poverty alleviation, community rebuilding, advancement, sustainability, and elimination of socioeconomic inequalities. It also implies a fuller comprehension of charitable purposes such as prevention or relief of poverty, advancement of education, religion, health or saving lives, and citizenship or community development.

Following is the establishment of relationships among the concepts so as to inform a model for the evaluation of ethical aspects of philanthropic strategies employed by charitable organizations.

## Establishing Relationships among Concepts

Establishing relationships among concepts entails defining the concepts in such a way that they can no longer be viewed or treated in isolation, but in relation to each other and as parts of a bigger whole. When concepts are defined and viewed in relation to each other, they provide information about how empirical events occur, as well as how and why there is a relationship among the concepts.[10] The process involves identifying any concepts with multiple relationships with other concepts or if there are any current stand-alone concepts that can be associated with one another. As such, it is of necessity to determine the patterns and combination of patterns amongst the concepts and, to that effect, James Dickoff et al.'s survey list of questions has been employed and customized for the subject under study.[11] The questions are rephrased into more directly applicable than general terms as tabulated hereafter.

---

10. Dickoff et al., "Theory in a Practice Discipline," 431–33.
11. Dickoff et al., "Theory in a Practice Discipline," 434–35.

# MODEL FOR ETHICAL EVALUATION

## Establishing Relationships among Concepts

| S/A | Survey Question | Answer |
|---|---|---|
| 1 | Who is the agent responsible for philanthropic strategies? | Charitable organizations |
| 2 | Who is the recipient of philanthropic aid? | The local community members, irrespective of age, gender, race, ethnicity, or status. |
| 3 | What is the contextual reference wherein philanthropic strategies are employed by charitable organizations that are being evaluated? | Real-life context and naturalistic setting with diverse cultural aspects and community characteristics, where also philanthropic challenges and opportunities are experienced. |
| 4 | What are the techniques, procedures and/or protocols associated with evaluation of ethical aspects of philanthropic strategies? | Ethical reflection, community participation, defining community true needs, and implementing philanthropic strategies. |
| 5 | What is the aim of evaluating ethical aspects of philanthropic strategies? | To alleviate the plight of the poor and less privileged local people in an ethically acceptable manner. |
| 6 | What is the source of energy that provides motivation for the evaluation of ethical aspects of philanthropic strategies employed by charitable organizations? | The lack of policy framework and ethical guidelines to govern and guide charitable organizations in the local community and country at large. For example, Zambia as a country has had no policy to govern charitable organizations from precolonial times. |
| 7 | When will the facilitation of evaluation of ethical aspects of philanthropic strategies employed by charitable organizations in the local communities be terminated? | When community participation and ethicality become evident among recipients; that is, when they are able to participate in the formulation, implementation, and evaluation of philanthropic strategies employed by charitable organizations in their communities. |

Following is a discussion of the foregoing tabulated relationships among the concepts and the practical relevance thereof for the community.

## Agent of Philanthropic Strategies

As stated in the issue that triggered the research for this book, charitable organizations have an obligation to foster ethics in their philanthropic strategies, given their public service mission. According to Hasnan et al., ethics may even be more important for charitable than non-charitable organizations.[12] Said another way, one can argue that charitable organizations have an even bigger stake in creating and maintaining an ethically positive public image than private enterprises because their primary stakeholders are donors.

I accept, for the purpose of this study, that charitable organizations have a critical role to play in the development of society, improvement of communities, and promotion of citizen participation.[13] The scope of this book, however, is to evaluate the praxis and impact of ethical aspects of philanthropic strategies employed by charitable organizations in improving the lives of the local people and community at large in specific areas. This calls for ethical reflection on the part of charitable organizations, which is the use of ethical principles, rules, or guidelines to direct action toward moral ends.[14] This is not a matter of importing ethics into a research or problematic praxis, but rather the recognition that ethical norms and values already are part of any project process.[15] And the application of such norms and values does not only occur at the end of a project, but is present from the outset and influences it right through the process as Don Browning also reckons.[16] As it were, "Ethicality" in this case is seen as a desired means of effecting philanthropic strategies by charitable organizations.

That is where the model I propose in this book endeavors to make a notable contribution to social work perspectives. What the model then proceeds to do is to provide guidelines of how the charitable organizations as agents of philanthropic strategies can best direct their efforts and resources toward alleviating the plight of the poor in an ethically acceptable manner.

One of the critical things that charities ought to do always is to ensure community participation.

---

12. Hasnan et al., *Issues, Challenges,* 777.
13. Candid, "What Is an NGO?"
14. Osmer, *Practical Theology,* 161.
15. Osmer, *Practical Theology,* 149.
16. Browning, *Fundamental Practical Theology,* 39.

## Model for Ethical Evaluation

### Ensure Community Participation from the Outset and Throughout

The success and sustainability of any community project also inextricably depends on community participation in the project planning, implementation, and ongoing decision-making. The aspect of community participation resonates throughout this book. Right from the issue that triggered the research, it is clear that charitable organizations have a critical role to play in the promotion of citizen participation in poverty alleviation undertakings such as philanthropy.[17] As such, it is imperative for local communities to fully participate in both the formulation and implementation of philanthropic strategies intended for them, rather than being merely recipients of foreign concepts without due adherence to the autonomous identity and dynamics of their local contexts. Charitable organizations should, therefore, ensure that their strategies and everything they do to help individuals and communities is interwoven into the structures and systems of the respective communities so that it can be utilized and sustained by the local people beyond the life of the projects in the communities.

Community participation enhances sustainability of transformational development triggered by philanthropic strategies and activities.

### Sustainability

This is also inextricably implicit in the evaluation of ethical aspects of philanthropic strategies employed by charitable organizations right from ethical reflection on charitable organizations and purposes. Accordingly, philanthropic strategies such as welfare approaches should not disempower local people and cause dependency as Sarah Blackman also reckons.[18] Rather, the focus should be on increasing self-reliance of the local people such as through income generation initiatives. Therefore, the local communities must pay attention to the incentives and philanthropic strategies that enable local households to adjust their production systems and livelihoods in ways that guarantee both welfare and sustainable economic growth.[19] This would also ensure sustainable development strategies without compromising the local people's identity and rights such as self-determination.

---

17. Candid, "What Is an NGO?"
18. Blackman, *Partnering with the Local Church*, 30–32.
19. Pender et al., "Strategies for Sustainable Development," 1.

One of the major reasons for the failure by charitable organizations to impact the community is a lack of sustainability in terms of continuity of both expert support staff and strategy implementation. It also became evident from the interviews that the charitable organizations overly depended or relied entirely on external aid, which was not sustainable. The local community is expected to utilise philanthropic aid to help individuals and communities attain sustainable transformational development through technical, physical, and financial support to enhance bigger and long-term transformational projects as Van Hoek and Sue Yardley[20] also observe.

For instance, the problem of climate change as identified by the local people of Mongu and elsewhere on earth calls for the preservation of the ecosystem and sustainable utilization of natural resources as an ethical obligation of every person on earth. As such, it is inevitable for the agents of philanthropic strategies to also do due diligence to sustainability as an inextricably implicit ethical issue.

## Recipient of Philanthropic Aid

The recipients of philanthropic aid are the local community as a whole irrespective of age, gender, race, ethnicity, or status diversity of its people. The research highlighted the vulnerable (children, youth, women, old age, differently abled), deserving poor, and other less privileged people in society, and that was sufficiently representative.

In general, within the context of social work, which is the conceptual framework of the scope of this book, the goals of philanthropy in developing countries are to help communities rebuild, advance, become sustainable, and eliminate social and economic inequality.[21] In particular, within the scope of this book, the concept of philanthropic strategy entails alleviating the plight of the poor and less privileged African people in an ethically acceptable manner.[22] As such, "ethicality" in this case is seen as a desired means of effecting philanthropic strategies of charitable organizations.

It is, therefore, expected that most African communities and charitable organizations will benefit from the evaluation of the ethical aspects of philanthropic strategies employed by charitable organizations such as operated in Mongu district of Western Zambia. As such, it is practically

20. Hoek and Yardley, *Keeping Communities Clean*, 6.
21. Burgess-Van Aken, "Goals of Philanthropy."
22. Magnus, *Age of Aging*, 136.

relevant for the local community as the recipient of philanthropic aid to also have some pre-requisite skills and capacity to work with charitable organizations that come to operate in their communities.

## Community Capacity Building

As it were, capacity building is central to the quest for sustainable community transformation and co-goal of technical assistance, not just a mere component or by-product of development programs.[23] It entails growing local institutions and organizations with the vision, will, wisdom, and skills to work together to build a more prosperous, equitable, just, and sustainable community.[24] Furthermore, capacity building encompasses a community's human, scientific, technological, organizational, institutional, and resource capabilities.[25] For philanthropic strategies to be ethically and sustainably impactful, they ought to be equally accompanied by community capacity building. During the interviews, some participants also seemed to be aware of the fact that any meaningful philanthropic strategy should equally consider community capacity building as an essential component.

Without capacity building, there can be no sustainability of transformational development projects initiated by philanthropic strategies.

## Contextual Reference of Philanthropic Strategies

Philanthropic strategies are applied in real-life contexts and naturalistic settings with diversity of cultures and community characteristics, where also philanthropic challenges and opportunities can be experienced. It is in contexts such as this that social work engages actively with a broader spectrum of other fields and endeavors to adopt their theories and method for its own use—that is regarding help for the client, as Michal Opatrný writes.[26] This also helps the social worker to come up with meaningful interpretations of perceived patterns and behaviors of clients. According to Etresia Evans, working with people in a social, naturalistic, and indeed holistic approach requires one to look at the person from a whole-life perspective because

23. Kaniaru et al., *Capacity Building*, 10.
24. MDC, *Alleghany Foundation*, 9.
25. Kaniaru et al., *Capacity Building*, 11.
26. Opatrný, "Caritas Theory," 300.

systems are nestled within other systems in the web of life.[27] As such, the subject hereby under study has the potential to contribute significantly to social work perspectives with regard to ethics in philanthropy from the unique context of the ethical aspects of philanthropic strategies employed by charitable organizations operating in a typical African community.

*Understand the Community through Community Research*

It is important to understand the community through research before moving in with a philanthropic strategy because community is a complex context. Therefore, as part of formulating philanthropic strategies, charitable organizations should conduct community research in order to understand the surrounding dynamics and systems, as well as accurately determine the true needs of the people. As Rick Warren writes, the best way to find out the culture, mind-set, and lifestyle of a people is to talk to them.[28] This is also in accordance with the overall aim of a qualitative research such as this, which is to understand the actions and practices in which humans engage in everyday life and the meaning that they ascribe to their lived experiences.[29] All else being equal, no pre-community research can result in failure of a project or community members opposing the project. It was evident from the empirical research interviews that participants expected charitable organizations first to understanding the community through research before determining what type of help they should offer and strategy to employ.

### Techniques Associated with Evaluating Ethics in Philanthropy

As highlighted in the section on "Agent of Philanthropic Strategies," the model proposed in this book focuses on ethical reflection and then proceeds to give guidelines on how to best direct efforts and resources towards ethical philanthropy. As such, the techniques associated with ethics in philanthropy are: *community participation, defining community true needs, and enacting philanthropic strategies*. As it were, community participation is not separable from the success and sustainability of philanthropic strategies. On defining community true needs, suffice it to state that these should be

---

27. Evans, "Theological Perspective," 5; Osmer, *Practical Theology*, 119.
28. Warren, *Purpose Driven Church*, 66.
29. Osmer, *Practical Theology*, 49–50.

holistic and concrete felt needs of the community and local communities are actually more effective in defining and meeting their own true needs than external helpers.[30] As such, they should not be left out of the process of identifying and defining their true needs. Enacting philanthropic strategies should aim at addressing the true needs of the community in an ethically acceptable manner, and the local people should be involved. Suffice it to add that determining the real purpose of an organization claiming to be a charity will also help to evaluate whether the organization is really doing charity or not, as its purpose will be weighed against charitable purposes and other relevant ethical frameworks.

## Aim of Philanthropic Strategies

The aim of philanthropic strategies within the particular scope of this book is to alleviate the plight of the poor and less privileged people in society through ethically acceptable means as earlier stated.[31] This is in tandem with the overall goals of philanthropy in developing countries, namely, to help communities rebuild, advance, become sustainable, and eliminate social and economic inequality.[32]

## Source of Energy Providing Motivation for Evaluation of Ethics in Philanthropic Strategies

The source of energy that provides motivation for the evaluation of ethics in philanthropic strategies of charitable organizations is the dire need for policy framework and ethical guidelines to govern and guide philanthropic strategies of NGOs in Zambia and the rest of Africa. As stated in the introduction of this book, even as a country, Zambia had no national policy to govern the NGO sector, which included charities, despite the influx of NGOs in the country from pre-colonial times.[33] Therefore, it was not known to what extent the ethical obligations of charitable organizations in the country were honored or dishonored in the implementation of their philanthropic strategies. The last cited government source as per footnote

---

30. Gabriel, *Human Factor in Rural Development*, 4.
31. Magnus, *Age of Aging*, 136.
32. Burgess-Van Aken, "Goals of Philanthropy."
33. MCDSS, *NGO File 2018*, 1–2.

was the first and only exclusive policy document so far on the governance of NGOs in Zambia published in April 2018, although it was still undergoing review and did not contain an explicit ethical code of conduct for NGOs operating in the country. There is, therefore, a definite concrete felt need to have a form of evaluation for the ethical aspects of philanthropic strategies employed by charitable NGOs in the country.

As it were, research findings are valid within their specific time, space, and value context, but as Nancy Burns and Susan Grove also observe, understanding the meaning of a phenomenon in its context makes it easier to understand phenomena in other similar contexts.[34] This is particularly applicable in the case of the subject of this book as the issue that triggered the study is symmetrical with what is going on in the rest of the country and most parts of Africa, if not the whole world. Therefore, there is a definite gap for which this book is purposed to make a positive contribution.

## Termination of Facilitating Evaluation of Ethics in Philanthropic Strategies of Charitable Organizations

Termination of an activity is linked to the achievement of its aim, which in this case is the alleviation of the plight of the poor and less privileged people in society in an ethically acceptable manner. As it were, the goals of philanthropy are to help communities rebuild, advance, become sustainable, and eliminate social and economic inequality. In other words, it implies an augmented holistic evolution of the quality of life of the local people, meaning that it never really ends, but rather evolves, because contexts and data of society are constantly evolving, too.[35] The process of facilitating the implementation of the model hereby proposed is, however, meant to enhance ethical evaluation of philanthropic strategies of charitable NGOs, which also gives the recipients the ability to participate in the formulation and implementation of philanthropic strategies meant for them. Therefore, it can be inferred that the process of facilitating the implementation of the model proposed in this book would be terminated when the evaluation of ethical aspects of philanthropic strategies by charitable organizations becomes evident in the community and charitable organizations. As Tom Gabriel states, the momentum towards further developments depends on

34. Botes, "Functional Approach," 22; Burns and Grove, *Practice of Nursing Research*, 29.

35. Osmer, *Practical Theology*, 75; University of Exeter, "Human Societies."

## Model for Ethical Evaluation

knowledge of the local people and their effects upon current developmental efforts.[36]

## Relationship Statements

Relationship statements derive from the development of the relationships among concepts and usually give an indication of the structure of the developing model. Therefore, in view of the foregoing relationship among concepts, the following relationship statements apply:

i. The agent of philanthropy (charitable organization) is responsible for ethics in philanthropic strategies and should, therefore, ensure ethical reflection from the outset and throughout the whole process because ethics are inseparably part and parcel of philanthropy. Furthermore, the charitable organization should also see to it that all its strategies are interwoven into the structures and systems of the respective community so that they can be utilized and sustained by the local community beyond the life of the project in the community.

ii. The recipient of philanthropic aid is the local community as a whole, irrespective of the ages, genders, races, or statuses of its people who have their own individual and common true needs. As such, it is important for the agent—charitable organization—to understand the holistic needs of the community through community research so as to design and implement a philanthropic strategy that will address a true need of the community in a holistic manner.

iii. The context in which philanthropic strategies are employed is a real-lifelong naturalistic setting with diverse cultural characteristics and challenges. As such, a charitable organization needs to have a bird's eye view of what is going on in the community in order to ethically formulate and implement an appropriate philanthropic strategy. In this regard, it is imperative for the charitable organization to conduct community research before moving into the community with a philanthropic agenda.

iv. The techniques involved in the process are ethical reflection, community participation, defining community true needs (holistic real pressing felt needs), as well as formulating and implementing

---

36. Gabriel, *Human Factor in Rural Development*, 4.

philanthropic strategies. Therefore, a charitable organization should work together with the local community to see to it that the techniques associated with ethics in philanthropy are fundamentally incorporated in the whole process, and this will also lead to the creation of a model for evaluating philanthropic strategies employed by charitable organizations in the community.

v. The whole aim of evaluating ethics in philanthropy is to help towards alleviating the plight of the poor and less privileged people in society in an ethically acceptable manner. In a broader sense, it is to help communities rebuild, advance, become sustainable, and eliminate social and economic inequality.

vi. Hence the common underlying need for policy framework and ethical guidelines to govern and guide the philanthropic strategies of NGOs in the country is what provides motivation for the evaluation of ethical aspects of philanthropic strategies of charitable organizations.

vii. For the sake of effectiveness, a representative work group (for example, eight to twelve people) would purposively be selected from among members of the community, NGOs, and government officers in line ministries to practically model out the evaluation of ethical aspects of philanthropic strategies of charitable organizations operating in their local community.

viii. The process of facilitating the implementation of the model proposed in this book will be terminated when the participants in the work group exhibit the ability to participate in the formulation, implementation, and evaluation of ethical aspects of philanthropic strategies employed by NGOs in their community. As it were, the momentum towards further developments depends on the knowledge and ability of the local people and their effects upon current developmental efforts.

ix. The author accepts the fact that this might be only a slice in time, but the facilitation would have achieved its objectives in the sense that the local people would have participated in the formulation, implementation, and evaluation of ethical aspects of charitable NGOs operating in their community. Furthermore, this achievement also ensures success and sustainability of the current and future projects because the momentum for future developments depends on knowledge that the local people have as well as their effects upon current developmental projects.

x. Evaluating ethics in philanthropy is an evolving lifelong process as contexts and data of society also evolve with time. Therefore, the proposed model also has the ability to evolve in order to effectively address the evolving contexts and data of society with passage of time.

So far, the practical guidelines for charitable organizations in respect of the insights drawn from the relationships among concepts reveal that the model proposed by the author in this book focuses on ethical reflection as the central and guiding concept for evaluating ethical aspects of philanthropic strategies employed by charitable organizations. This is also what anchors the model in an interdisciplinary perspective of social work, pastoral theology, and common law and provides its unique contribution to social work. The model also shows how social work contextually and practically engages with other communities of experience and interpretation such as pastoral theology and common law to guide the philanthropic strategies of charitable organizations towards holistic and ethically sound ends.[37]

## DESCRIBING THE MODEL

In research, a model can be referred to as a pictorial or graphic representation of key concepts of a phenomenon.[38] According to Louise Rosenblatt, a model is an abstraction or generalized pattern devised in order to think about a subject.[39] Unlike a strategy, which is the process used to approach a particular problem, a model is a more abstract way of schematizing a process so that the strategy can be generalized to solve similar problems in other similar situations.

Although relationships among concepts are expected to give an indication of the structure or form of a model, sometimes it is still a bit difficult to identify the structure even after establishing the relationships amongst concepts, especially if the relationships are complex and unclear. In such a case, some guiding questions, such as those proposed by Peggy Chinn and Maeona Kramer, can aid a researcher or author to structure a model as follows:

37. Browning, *Fundamental Practical Theology*, 36.
38. See CohenMiller, "How Would You Define a 'Model.'"
39. Rosenblatt, "Transactional Model," 1057.

i. Which relationship is most central?
  ii. What is the direction, strength, and quality of this relationship?
  iii. Can a model be drawn up to represent the structure of this relationship?
  iv. In what order does the relationship occur?
  v. Does this relationship consolidate or distinguish the concepts?[40]

As soon as the structure of the central relationship is defined, a researcher or author can start to incorporate other relationships within the structure. Questions that would aid this process are:

  i. How do the secondary relationships link to the central one?
  ii. Can all relationships be shown by the structure?
  iii. Does the structure take on a multiple form?
  iv. Have competitive or shared structures been suggested by the relationships?
  v. Can parts of the structure be illustrated through the use of diagrams?

As the relationships are explored, the structures of the model and the individual components will begin to emerge. A recognizable structure is essential to a theory because structure flows from relationships as Peggy Chinn and Maeona Kramer further observe.[41] Likewise, after establishing the major and secondary relationships, I will describe a structure to represent the model in its entire form. As a strategy to formulate the description of the model, I will make use of the following six questions as further suggested by Chinn and Kramer:

  i. What is the purpose of the model? (This question addresses why the model was formulated and reflects the context and the situation to which the model can apply).
  ii. What are the concepts of the model? (Questions the qualitative and quantitative dimensions of concepts).
  iii. How are the concepts defined? (This question focuses on the meaning of the concepts within the model and the empiric value of the concepts).

---

40. Chinn and Kramer, *Theory and Nursing*, 113–14.
41. Chinn and Kramer, *Theory and Nursing*, 115.

## Model for Ethical Evaluation

iv. What is the nature of the relationships? (How are concepts linked together?).

v. What is the structure of the model? (This question addresses the overall form of the conceptual relationships).

vi. On what assumptions is the model built? (This question addresses the basic truths that underline the theoretic reasoning of the study).[42]

The model will finally be evaluated by making use of the critical reflection on theory in accordance with Peggy Chinn and Maeona Kramer as well as Lorraine Walker and Kay Avant.[43] Accordingly, the fivefold criterion to be employed comprises clarity, simplicity, generality, accessibility, and importance. Following is a brief discussion of each of these criteria.

i. **Clarity:** Semantic clarity, semantic consistency, structural clarity, and structural consistency of the model are to be considered in evaluating the clarity of a model. Semantic clarity hereby implies that similar empiric realities will come to mind when different people read the model. This is achieved when the key concepts in a model are defined through minimal use of words and appropriate use of examples and diagrams. Semantic consistency happens when concepts of the model are used consistently with their definitions. Structural clarity becomes evident when concepts are interconnected and organized into a coherent whole, while structural consistency occurs when the structural forms within a model act as a conceptual map that enhances clarity.

ii. **Simplicity:** This is achieved by using the minimum elements and relationships in the structural diagram of the model, while the core concepts supporting the purpose of the model are self-evident.

iii. **Generality:** Generality of the model implies the extent to which the model can be implemented in a broader and similar situation as intended by the study initially. Generality also refers to the soundness of the research evidence as well as its scientific validity and social value.[44]

---

42. Chinn and Kramer, *Theory and Nursing*, 117.

43. Chinn and Kramer, *Theory and Nursing*, 126–37; Walker and Avant, *Strategies for Theory Construction*, 135.

44. TRREE, *Introduction to Research Ethics*, 8.

iv. **Accessibility:** The model and theory generated through the research should be useful in promoting the goal of the model, namely the evaluation of ethical aspects of philanthropic strategies employed by charitable organizations.

v. **Importance:** The importance of a model has to do with its applicability and practical value, because the aim of social research is to make valuable contributions to organizations and communities.[45] By implication, there ought to be a rational relationship between explanatory theory and empirical evidence of the study.[46]

## Overview of the Model

The model presented compresses the concepts and relationship amongst concepts that have resulted from a critical pragmatic synthesis of all the preceding research tasks with regard to the subject matter herein explored. As it were, the conducting of a research must construct its own theory.[47] As such, a description of the structure and process of the model is provided, as well as its operationalization.

The overview of the model is hereby presented, which I refers to as *Decent Aid* and its structural explanation follows afterwards.

---

45. Yarbrough et al., *Program Evaluation Standards*.
46. Payne, *Modern Social Work Theory*, 4.
47. Bamberger et al., *RealWorld Evaluation*, 301; Bryant and Charmaz, *SAGE Handbook of Grounded Theory*, 253.

# Model for Ethical Evaluation

## Purpose of the Model

The purpose of the model is to provide a framework that will guide communities and charitable organizations in evaluating the ethical aspects of philanthropic strategies employed by charitable organizations operating in various communities, especially in Africa. This is an important aspect because ethics in philanthropy is a subject that is usually shrouded in darkness, so to say. As it were, the goals of philanthropy within social work are to help communities rebuild, advance, become sustainable, and eliminate social and economic inequality as earlier mentioned. Therefore, the model focuses on the evaluation of ethical aspects of philanthropic strategies by charitable organizations to enhance ethical community upliftment. As such, ethical reflection is perceived to be the central concept in evaluating the ethicality of philanthropic strategies employed by the charitable organizations.

The ethical evaluation process is also based on the concept of community participation as identified in the issue that triggered the research for this book, empirical research results, as well as it being a technique associated with ethical evaluation of philanthropic strategies by charities. Accordingly, the sustainability of any community project also inextricably depends on community participation in the project planning, implementation, and decision-making. Therefore, it is inevitable that charitable organizations should ensure full community participation from the outset in planning and implementing philanthropic strategies. The whole process builds on community participation and revolves around ethical reflection throughout.

## Definition of Concepts in the Model

It is imperative to define the concepts in the model in order to develop a robust and intelligible description of the model. Accordingly, the concepts in the model comprise the central and associated concepts, or primary and secondary concepts, as hereafter presented and defined.

### Ethical Reflection as the Central Concept

"Ethical reflection" is central to evaluation of ethics in philanthropy as per the model hereby proposed. For instance, it is unethical to implement any philanthropic strategy without the community participating in identifying their true needs. As it were, "ethical reflection" is the use of ethical principles, rules, or guidelines to guide action toward moral ends.[48] As already recapitulated, this is not a matter of importing ethics into a project or problematic praxis, but rather the recognition that ethical norms and values already are part of any project process, which in this case is any philanthropic strategy. As such, the application of such ethical norms should not only occur at the end of the project, but ought to be present from the outset and influence the project throughout. Hence ethical reflection is the central concept in the model.

As such, even if a country has no policy to govern NGOs, it is still possible and imperative to evaluate the ethical aspects of philanthropic strategies employed by charitable organizations in its communities through ethical reflection with universal ethical principles. In turn, the respective organizations and moral communities can test their practices and norms against universally acceptable ethical standards as Richard Osmer also reckons.[49]

Everything else in the model revolves around ethical reflection. What the model then proceeds to do is to give guidelines of how the reflection on universal ethical principles and standards can best guide philanthropic efforts and resources by incorporating other significantly related concepts from the synthesis of the preceding research tasks.

## Community Participation

From the perspective of social work, community participation is the foundational principal of any community transformation process.[50] Right from the initial problematic issue it is clear that charitable organizations have a critical role to play in the promotion of citizen participation in developmental undertakings such as philanthropic strategies.[51] As already stated, it is imperative for local communities to fully participate in both the formulation and implementation of philanthropic strategies intended for them, rather than merely trying out foreign concepts without due adherence to their autonomous identity and local context dynamics. Charitable

48. Osmer, *Practical Theology*, 161.
49. Osmer, *Practical Theology*, 49.
50. Tesoriero, *Community Development*, 144.
51. Candid, "What Is an NGO?"

organizations should, therefore, ensure that their strategies and everything they do to help individuals and communities is interwoven into the structures and systems of the respective communities so that they can be utilized and sustained by the local community beyond the life of the project in the community.

Lack of community participation in the charities' philanthropic strategies was also identified as one of the main reasons the charitable organizations failed to make positive impact in the communities where they operated as per empirical research results. As a foundational principal, community participation holds together and sustains the process and efforts of any philanthropic strategy. As such, the evaluation of ethical aspects of philanthropic strategies is also based on community participation as earlier identified in the problematic issue and empirical research. Accordingly, the sustainability of any community project inextricably depends on community participation in the project planning, implementation, and decision-making. As with ethical reflection, charitable organizations should ensure full community participation from the outset in the formulation and implementation of philanthropic strategies. As it were, the whole process builds on community participation and revolves around ethical reflection. This is clearly depicted in the model hereby presented.

## True Needs

These must be concrete felt needs by the local people themselves, not only by a specialist external expert. Key to effective philanthropic strategies is accurate understanding of the true needs of the target population or community.[52] As such, needs identification is a pre-requisite for action and local people must be involved in identifying their own needs.[53] Just as community transformation is about addressing the true needs of the affected people, so is ethical philanthropy.

During the interviews, participants expressed their real pressing problems and felt needs, but it was also clear that the charitable organizations did little to ensure that their philanthropic strategies addressed the true needs of the local people in the communities. Some participants further expected

52. Gautier, "Building a Philanthropic Strategy"; Sticker, "True Need in Kant," 432–34.

53. Adejunmobi, "Self-Help Community Development," 226; Jeppe, *Community Development*, 28.

the charitable organizations to conduct thorough research to identify the real pressing problems and felt needs of the people rather than just moving in with philanthropic strategies that did not address their true needs.

A common problem in community transformation strategies such as philanthropy is who determines what the needs are. As Tom Gabriel writes, the momentum towards another development depends upon knowledge of indigenous power structures and their effects upon current developmental efforts.[54] Outsiders assuming responsibility for planning, funding, and implementation of developmental activities such as philanthropic strategies usually display scant knowledge of how their target communities live. It is, therefore, important that indigenous knowledge of human thought and behaviour is taken into consideration when identifying community needs and this is only possible if the local people are involved in identifying their own true needs from the outset.

*Aid Strategy*

As earlier stated, within the context of the research for this book, the concept of philanthropic strategies entails alleviating the plight of the poor and less privileged people in society through ethically acceptable means.[55] Therefore, ethicality is seen as the desired means of effecting philanthropic strategies by charitable organizations.

Suffice it to recapitulate that the relevance of any community transformation strategy, which in this case is philanthropy, is tied to the true needs of the particular community that it seeks to help.[56] As such, a relevant philanthropic strategy should actually address the real concrete felt needs of the target community through ethically acceptable means and standards.

## Explanation of the Structure of the Model

To aid the explanation of the structure of the model, it will be considered in its constituent parts and remarks will be made on each respective part.

---

54. Gabriel, *Human Factor in Rural Development*, 4.
55. Mahrik, "End Justifies the Means," 136.
56. Swanepoel and Beer, *Community Development*, 47.

## Model for Ethical Evaluation

### Ethical Reflection

Just as centrally positioned in the model, ethical reflection is the central concept and motivating factor for the evaluation of ethical aspects of philanthropic strategies implemented by charitable organizations. Even where there is no policy to govern NGOs, it is still imperative to evaluate the ethical aspects of philanthropic strategies employed by charitable organizations through ethical reflection with universal ethical principles in order to allow the respective organizations and moral communities to test their practices and norms against universally acceptable ethical standards. So, it all starts, revolves, and evolves around ethical reflection! The rest are significantly associated concepts that anchor and revolve around the central concept and assist to make effective the evaluation of the ethical aspects of philanthropic strategies employed by charitable organizations.

### Community Participation

Community participation is strategically positioned at the baseline in the model because it is the foundational principal of any community transformation process.[57] The sustainability of any community project also fundamentally depends and builds on community participation in the project planning, implementation, and decision making.[58] As such, it is imperative that the model builds on community participation in order to be sustainable and capable of addressing new or futuristic challenges.

### True Needs and Aid Strategy

Key to effective philanthropic strategy is accurate identification and understanding of the true needs of the target population or community.[59] This is a pre-requisite for action and local people must be involved in identifying their own needs. As it were, philanthropy is all about addressing true needs of the people as per Kantian ethics.[60] Therefore, the relevance of any community transformation strategy, which in this case is philanthropy, is tied to the concrete felt needs of the particular community that it seeks to address.

---

57. Tesoriero, *Community Development*, 144.
58. Abiche, "Community Development Initiatives," 27.
59. Gautier, "Building a Philanthropic Strategy."
60. Cf. Sticker, "True Need in Kant," 432–34.

In the model, community true needs and aid strategy converge because there can be no ethical or indeed any meaningful philanthropic strategy that is not 'bent' towards addressing community true needs. That is why at the bottom of it the local community should be participating fully even in the identification of their own needs and aid strategy formulation for the whole process to be ethical, effective and sustainable.

*Termination of Facilitation of the Evaluation Process*

As it were, evaluation of ethical aspects of philanthropic strategies itself is a continuous process as long as charitable organizations are operating in communities. However, in the case of a project where the model is implemented, the process of facilitating the implementation of the model presented in this book would be terminated when the evaluation of ethical aspects of philanthropic strategies becomes evident in the community and charitable organizations. As an indicator, at this stage it is expected that the participants will also have the ability to participate in the formulation and implementation of philanthropic strategies employed by charitable organizations in their communities so as to be able to appropriately evaluate the ethicality of the strategies employed. This is a prerequisite for the termination because the momentum towards further developments depends on knowledge of the local people and their effects upon current developmental efforts.[61]

## Assumptions of the Model

Assumptions are basic "givens" or accepted truths that are fundamental to a model and they may take the form of factual assertions or reflect value positions.[62] Accordingly, factual assertions are statements that are based on or affirm facts, while value positions refer to what is viewed as right, good, or what ought to be. According to Walter Borg and others, all research is value-laden, and instead of trying to avoid the issue of value, a researcher needs to make these values very clear.[63] Likewise, the assumptions of the model are hereby provided.

61. Gabriel, *Human Factor in Rural Development*, 4.
62. Chinn and Kramer, *Theory and Nursing*, 116.
63. Borg et al., *Applying Educational Research*, 197.

## Model for Ethical Evaluation

i. The primary assumption of the model hereby proposed is that an evaluation of ethical aspects of philanthropic strategies employed by charitable organizations will enhance ethicality and professionalism of the charitable organizations and optimize benefits to the local community through ethically acceptable means. This assumption is also in tandem with the hypothesis of the scope of this book.

ii. The central concept in the development of a model for evaluating ethical aspects of philanthropic strategies by charitable organizations is ethical reflection with universal ethical principles and standards.

iii. The agent of ethics in philanthropy is any charitable organization that operates in a given area or community.

iv. The energy that provides motivation for the evaluation of ethical aspects of philanthropic strategies by charitable organizations is that there is insufficient policy (if any) to govern charitable organizations in the local context of the research, which is also the case with the wider context such as the country of Zambia and most parts of the African continent.

v. The community's true needs as expressed by participants in the research provide further motivation to engage with the charities in coming up with a model for evaluating the ethical aspects of philanthropic strategies by charitable organizations.

vi. Facilitating the evaluation of philanthropic strategies by charitable organizations involves ethical reflection as the central concept, community participation as a foundational principle, as well as community true needs being met by corresponding philanthropic strategies.

vii. In the process of implementation, the charitable organization also enhances its ethicality and professionalism.

viii. Evaluation of ethical aspects of charities is a lifelong process. As such, facilitating the implementation of the model represents only a slice in time, as it would take too long to determine the success of the evaluation process in the long term. In spite of this, a pilot implementation of the model would succeed in achieving its objectives as the community participants would gain experience and ability to participate in the formulation, implementation, and evaluation of philanthropic strategies employed by charitable organizations in their communities, which will in turn ensure success and sustainability of similar projects in future.

## EVALUATING THE MODEL

Peer review, member checking, and triangulation of data and data sources were identified as mechanisms to bolster credibility of the research for this book. These, together with Chinn and Kramer's criteria, namely: clarity, simplicity, generality, accessibility, and importance have been used to evaluate the model.[64]

### Peer Review

With regards to peer review, the whole study process leading up to the construction of the model was overseen by a study promoter, an expert in social work and pastoral theology, as well as several others who provided professional guidance in various seminars that informed the study.

### Member Checking

During member checking, participants confirmed the reasonableness of the researcher's interpretations drawn from the data. The researcher thanked the participants and thus made known to them the empirical research findings too.

### Triangulation

On triangulation, suffice it to state that the model has been constructed from a synthesis of the concepts developed from the data and data sources of all the research tasks involved. Furthermore, it is also informed by two theories that are relevant to the topic under study according to the empirical research results and broader literature survey as well as scope of the research, which meets the criteria for triangulation and bolsters credibility of the resultant model.

---

64. Chinn and Kramer, *Theory and Nursing*, 137.

## Clarity

Clarity of the model entails meaningful and consistent usage of ideas and concepts within the model. In order to meet this criterion, all the concepts in this model have been defined and linked in such a way that their relationships are clearly understood. The definitions and their structural forms have been used consistently and were continuously evaluated to ensure that semantic and structural clarity are preserved.

## Simplicity

This is evidenced by the minimum use of elements in the model as the main concepts sufficiently support the purpose of the model and are self-evident. No new or unimportant concepts from outside the study were introduced at this stage.

## Generality

Generality hereby implies the extent to which the model can be implemented in a broader and similar situation as initially intended by the study. As evidenced by the guiding concepts in the model itself, this model can be implemented in other broader similar situations, whether in rural or urban settings. For instance, the central concept of ethical reflection is universal, and so are the significantly associated concepts of community participation, community true needs, and philanthropic strategy.

The concept of generality also entails the social value or usefulness as well as scientific validity and rigour of the constructed model. As such, I am under the impression that this model will contribute to the understanding of social work with regard to ethics in philanthropy, especially from the unique context of the charitable organizations operating in typical African communities such as Mongu in Western Zambia. As it were, research findings are valid within their specific time, space, and value context, but also understanding the meaning of a phenomenon in its context makes it rather easier to understand phenomena in other similar contexts.[65]

---

65. Botes, "Functional Approach," 22; Burns and Grove, *Practice of Nursing Research*, 29.

Finally on this criterion, the inclusive nature of the model also enables it to evolve and attend to new or futuristic challenges pertaining to ethics in philanthropy as the contexts and data of society evolve over time.

## Accessibility

The model and respective theory generated through this book are useful in promoting ethics in philanthropy. The model focuses on the evaluation of ethical aspects of philanthropic strategies employed by charitable organizations, which, as agents of philanthropy, should reflect on universal ethical principles and standards in the formulation and implementation of their philanthropic strategies. For instance, it would be unethical to embark on a philanthropic strategy without addressing the community's true needs. Hence the great contribution of this model to the field of philanthropic social work is its focus on ethical reflection as the central concept in evaluating ethical aspects of philanthropic strategies employed by charitable organizations.

## Importance

The importance of a model has to do with its applicability and practical value. As per its design, this book is about evaluating ethical aspects of philanthropic strategies of charitable organizations and, as indicated from the outset, it has been prompted by the lack of sufficient policy framework to guide and govern charitable organizations in the country. Accordingly, results of the empirical research strongly confirm the researcher's supposition in this chapter of the book, namely, to develop action-guiding concepts aimed at developing a new praxis and model that will guide the evaluation of ethical aspects of philanthropic strategies of charitable organizations.

Furthermore, member checking and peer review during data collection and final reflection on the whole process have also served to ensure that the development of the model was credible, relevant, and applicable.

As such, the model is hereby considered to be important because it has potential to yield positive and practical results in the context where it was developed and other similar contexts.

# Model for Ethical Evaluation

## SUMMARY PERSPECTIVES ON CHAPTER 6

In this chapter, I have endeavoured to develop and present a new praxis and model to guide the evaluation of ethical aspects of philanthropic strategies of charitable organizations. As it were, theory in social work does not only inform practice but is also developed from practice and, therefore, it is also evidence-based. Therefore, discussions of empirical research findings have been connected with theoretical perspectives in the broader research in order to promote evidence-informed practice with theory-informed practice. As such, this chapter has focused on developing a model for evaluating ethical aspects of philanthropic strategies employed by charitable organizations based on both empirical and theoretical discourses of the respective study.

Firstly, a summary of perspectives from the preceding theoretical and empirical tasks was presented so as to establish a guiding framework for the development of action-guiding concepts that led to a new praxis and model to guide the evaluation of ethical aspects of philanthropic strategies employed by charitable organizations. Accordingly, a synthesis of the preceding tasks with regard to the topic under study resulted into four main concepts, with several respective sub-concepts, that formed action-guiding concepts for evaluating ethical aspects of philanthropic strategies employed by charitable organizations.

In order to maintain the scientific rigour of the academic process, a brief discussion of the main concepts of the model and their respective sub-concepts has been presented. Furthermore, the relationship between concepts was established by adhering to proven guiding principles such as James Dickoff and others' survey list of questions, which in turn led to the description and construction of the model.[66]

An important factor of this book is that within social, which is the conceptual guiding framework of the underpinning study, the goals of philanthropy are to help communities rebuild, advance, become sustainable, and eliminate social and economic inequality. Therefore, the development of a model for the evaluation of ethical aspects of philanthropic strategies employed by charitable organizations is hereby seen as enhancing the ethicality and impact of the efforts of well-meaning charitable organizations and maximizing benefits to the local communities through ethically acceptable means.

---

66. Dickoff et al., "Theory in a Practice Discipline," 434–35.

Furthermore, this chapter has judiciously highlighted ethical reflection as the central concept in the evaluation of ethics in philanthropy. This is also what anchors the model within an intersection of social work, common law, and theological perspectives, and where it makes its unique contribution to social work. What the model then proceeds to do is to provide guidelines on how the charitable organizations can best direct their efforts and resources toward alleviating the plight of the poor in an ethically acceptable manner by integrating the other significantly related concepts. Finally, I have presented the structural explanation, assumptions, and evaluation of the constructed model for the evaluation of ethical aspects of philanthropic strategies employed by charitable organizations, which I call decent aid.

The last chapter will present the concluding perspectives with regard to the topic under study in this book.

# 7

# Concluding Perspectives

## INTRODUCTION

This final chapter provides valuable concluding perspectives regarding the ethical evaluation of philanthropic strategies employed by charitable organizations as explored, discussed and presented in this book. Just as Michael Coughlan et al. and Cynthia Russel also reckon, the discussion in the concluding part of a study should flow naturally and logically from the empirical data and be related to the respective explanatory theory.[1] I will, therefore, in this chapter provide a summary and evaluation of the study, limitations experienced, make recommendations, suggest areas for further research as emerged from the findings, and present final remarks.

## SUMMARY AND EVALUATION

The overall aim of the work of this book has been to evaluate the ethical aspects of philanthropic strategies employed charitable organizations operating among poor African communities such as Mongu district of Western Zambia. Accordingly, the research was prompted by the fact that next to nothing was known about the ethical aspects and operating strategies of charitable organizations in local communities despite an influx of such organizations in the area for about a century. Furthermore, even as a country, Zambia had no national policy to govern the NGO sector, which included

---

1. Coughlan et al., "Step-By-Step Guide"; Russell, "Evaluating Quantitative Research," 61–64.

charities, despite the influx of NGOs in the country since the precolonial era. It was, therefore, not known to what extent were the ethical obligations of charitable organizations honored or dishonored in the implementation of their philanthropic strategies. As such, it was not possible to address the issue at local level without connecting to what was happening at national level and the continent of Africa at large.

The study was conducted in a specific area where charitable organizations had been operating from precolonial times in order to endorse its relevance and practicality, because the aim of social research is to make valuable contributions to organizations and communities.

The foregoing background to the study strongly suggested the need for evaluating the ethical aspects of charitable organizations that operated in the local community and country and, by default, Africa as a continent.

As a prerequisite, the subject under investigation was contextualized by presenting background contexts that called for the study, as well as stating and explaining the issue. Both local and global trends that had resulted in a renewed interest in ethical aspects of philanthropic strategies of charitable organizations were discussed. As such, the purpose of undertaking the study was spelt out; the objectives, research questions, and the approach to be used have all been presented accordingly.

The concept of "philanthropic strategies" in this book and context of the backing research entails alleviating the plight of the poor and less privileged local people in an ethically acceptable manner. This is in accordance with the primary concept of philanthropy that is also upheld by religious teachings of human wellbeing, the good life, good society, and transformation of the world. "Ethicality" in this case is seen as a desired means of effecting philanthropic strategies of charitable organizations.

The respective theoretical framework has been based on an interdisciplinary perspective of theological and sociological discourses comprising pastoral theology, social work, and common law.

As a strategy of inquiry, I first had to determine, through literature review in the broader spectrum, theoretical perspectives that could enrich our understanding of ethical aspects of philanthropic strategies employed by charitable organizations that operated among poor African communities. Consequently, I had to operationalize the charitable organizations and conduct extensive literature survey as explicated in the second and third chapters, respectively.

## Concluding Perspectives

Second, I took time to conduct a systematic empirical case study research to discover perspectives that could be descriptive-empirical evidence of the ethical aspects of philanthropic strategies employed by charitable organizations operating among poor African communities such as Mongu district in Western Zambia. By understanding a phenomenon in a particular context, it becomes rather easier to understand similar phenomena in other similar contexts. As such, it was important to give the study a context in a typical Africa setting. The results and discussions of my empirical investigations constitute the larger part of the fifth chapter of this book.

Finally, I developed, through critical pragmatic reflection on the findings of the preceding literature and empirical investigations, a model to guide the ethical evaluation of philanthropic strategies employed by charitable organizations. As it were, real science requires that there should be some rational connection between explanatory theory and empirical data. As such, I am certain that the model herein presented can also be used to evaluate philanthropic strategies of charitable organizations in other similar wider contexts within and outside Zambia and Africa.

## LIMITATIONS

Despite the achievement of developing a model for evaluating ethical aspects of philanthropic strategies of charities, it is imperative to highlight that there were limitations that I experienced in my study as outlined hereafter.

### Non-Availability and Skepticism of Some Participants

Not all the targeted participants were available for the interviews, especially from among officials of charitable organizations, while some community members refused to be interviewed as individuals and opted to be interviewed in form of group discussions. As such, I had to conduct interviews with community members and officials who were available until data saturation occurred. It is thus not known what the views of those who were not present would have been and to what extent they would have influenced the discussions had they been available.

## Specific Literature Based on the Focus of My Study

No literature on ethics in philanthropy based on the local area of my study was available. As such, it is alleged that no other prior study had ever been conducted either on the topic of my study or on any philanthropic strategies in the town. As such, I relied mainly on the data I gathered as well as other relevant literature concerning philanthropic strategies employed by charitable organizations in general in order to achieve my objective.

It is, therefore, commonplace to speculate that the foregoing limitations could have inhibited valuable contributions to my investigation, but unfortunately, it was beyond my control as it would be unethical to try to extract information from people without their free prior informed consent. It is in this regard that I make appropriate recommendations hereafter.

## RECOMMENDATIONS

The following recommendations hereby apply:

i. The conducting of the research and development of the model is not enough on own its own to bring about the desired ethicality and professionalism of the philanthropic strategies employed by charitable organizations. There is need to practically implement the model in the actual context of the study and other selected similar contexts in order to endorse its practicality and usefulness and, ultimately, realize the desired ethicality regarding philanthropic strategies employed by charitable organizations operating among poor African communities.

ii. As the central concept of the model is ethical reflection with universal principles, there is need to sensitize and capacity-build the respective local communities with regard to their ethical obligations and rights pertaining to philanthropic strategies of charitable organizations that operate in their communities. This aspect also came out strongly from some participants during the empirical research.

iii. The community should establish proper moral and ethical grounds when dealing with charitable organizations in order to guide action towards morally sound ends. To do so, they need to be equipped with relevant skill and knowledge on how to work with charitable organizations and donor aid.

Concluding Perspectives

## IMPLICATIONS FOR FURTHER RESEARCH

I hereby make no absolute claim whatsoever that my study was exhaustive with regard to ethics in philanthropy because only data that were relevant to achieving the objectives of my study have been presented in this book. There is still need for further research, at least in the following areas, based on the research findings:

i. The role of the community in corporate philanthropy
ii. Philanthropic strategies for Africa
iii. Ubuntu as an African social thought and ethic for philanthropic social work in Africa.

## FINAL REMARKS

In this book I have dealt with the evaluation of ethical aspects of philanthropic strategies employed by charitable organizations operating among poor African communities such as Mongu district of Western Zambia, where the case study was conducted. The process focused on ethical reflection with universally acceptable ethical principles, mainly because Zambia as a country had no policy to govern or regulate charitable organizations despite an influx of such organizations from precolonial times.

The research process was thoroughly discussed in the respective chapters and it included the issue, approach, and results, through which the workings of the research were shown. The study followed a multi-method approach comprising interviews, field notes, observations, and triangulation in order to come up with a rich and meaningful description of the philanthropic strategies employed by charitable organizations such as operated in Mongu town and by default, Zambia as a country.

During the empirical investigation, participants overwhelmingly expressed dissatisfaction at the philanthropic strategies employed by charitable organizations in their communities. As such, there was need to review the praxis of the said charities and thus evaluate the ethicality of their philanthropic strategies. Although the study was only a slice in time, I am of the opinion that it has achieved its objectives in the sense that, as a model, the local people participated in the evaluation of the ethical aspects of philanthropic strategies employed by charitable organizations that operated in their communities.

Two relevant theories were engaged to ethically evaluate the philanthropic strategies of charitable organizations according to the empirical research results, namely, Kant's moral theory and African traditional Ubuntu philosophy. Consequently, the ethical evaluation overwhelmingly revealed that there were serious ethical violations inherent in the philanthropic strategies employed charitable organizations in the area.

In chapter 6, I endeavoured to develop and present a model for the evaluation of ethical aspects of philanthropic strategies of charitable NGOs. The process involved synthesizing the key concepts from all the preceding research tasks with regard to the topic under study, which resulted in the formation of action-guiding concepts that in turn informed a model for evaluating ethical aspects of philanthropic strategies employed by charitable organizations.

Finally, in this concluding chapter, I have presented the summary of the perspectives of the whole study, limitations experienced in the process, recommendations and implications for further research, and my final remarks.

# Bibliography

Abiche, Tefera Tarole. "Community Development Initiatives and Poverty Reduction." MA thesis, University of Western Cape, 2004.
Adejunmobi, A. "Self-Help Community Development in Selected Nigerian Rural Communities: Problems and Prospects." *Community Development Journal* 25 (1990) 225–35.
Adeyemo, Tokunboh, ed. *Africa Bible Commentary*. Nairobi: WordAlive, 2006.
African Parks. "Liuwa Plain." https://www.africanparks.org/the-parks/liuwa-plain.
Ajibo, Henry. *Values, Ethics and Principles of Social Work*. Nsukka: University of Nigeria, 2017.
Akhtar, Inaan. *Research in Social Science: Interdisciplinary Perspective*. 1st ed. New Delhi: Jamia Millia Islamia, 2016.
Akintola, Owolabi. "NGO Accountability and Sustainable Development in Nigeria." *Journal of Modern Accounting and Auditing* 7 (2011) 67–75.
Akpenpuun, Joyce Rumun. "Influence of Religious Beliefs on Healthcare Practice." *International Journal of Education and Research* 2 (2014) 27–48.
American Sociological Association (ASA). "Religion and Spirituality." *ASA*, n.d. https://www.asanet.org/topics/religion-and-spirituality.
Anfara, Vincent A., and Norma T. Mertz, eds. *Theoretical Frameworks in Qualitative Research*. Thousand Oaks, CA: Sage, 2006.
Arendt, Hannah. *The Human Condition*. Chicago: University of Chicago Press, 1958.
Ascot Day Centre. "Six Types of Charitable Organisations." https://web.archive.org/web/20190905002747/http://ascotdaycentre.co.uk/types-of-charity-organizations/6-types-of-charity-organizations.
Aspers, Patrik, and Ugo Corte. "What Is Qualitative in Qualitative Research?" *Qualitative Sociology* 42 (2019) 139–60.
Atan, Ruhaya, et al. *Quality Information by Charity Organisations and Its Relationship with Donations*. Selangor: Universiti Teknolog MARA, 2012.
Austin, Michal. "Identifying the Conceptual Foundations of Practice Research." In *The Routledge Handbook of Social Work Practice Research*, edited by Lynette Joubert and Martin Webber, 15–31. London: Taylor and Francis, 2020.
Ayodele, Thompson, et al. *African Perspectives on Aid: Foreign Assistance Will Not Pull Africa Out of Poverty*. Washington, DC: Cato Institute of Economic Development, 2005.
BA Theories. "Kant's Ethical Theory: Kantian Ethics, Categorical Imperatives, Morality." https://www.batheories.com/kantian-ethics.

# Bibliography

Bamberger, Michael, et al. *RealWorld Evaluation: Working Under Budget, Time, Data, and Political Constraints.* 2nd ed. Thousand Oaks: SAGE, 2012.

Banks, Nicola, and David Hulme. *The Role of NGOs and Civil Society in Development and Poverty Reduction.* Working Paper 171. Manchester: Brooks World Poverty Institute, 2012.

Banks, Sarah J. "Social Work Ethics." In *International Encyclopedia of the Social and Behavioural Sciences,* edited by Neil J. Smelser and Paul B. Baltes, 22. 2nd ed. Oxford: Elsevier, 2015.

Barbie, Earl, and Johann Mouton. *The Practice of Social Research.* Cape Town: Oxford University Press, 2001.

Belcher, John, and Marcela Sarmiento Mellinger. "Integrating Spirituality with Practice and Social Justice: The Challenge for Social Work." *Journal of Religion & Spirituality in Social Work* 35.4 (2016) 377–94.

Benedict XVI. *Deus Caritas Est: On Christian Love.* Vatican City: Libreria Editrice Vaticana, 2006.

Berg, Bruce. *Qualitative Research Methods for the Social Sciences.* 5th ed. Boston: Pearson, 2004.

Beyer, Hermann W. "Diakonew, Diakonia, Diakonos." In *Theological Dictionary of the New Testament,* edited by Gerhard Kittel and Geoffrey W. Bromiley, 81–92. Grand Rapids: Eerdmans, 1964.

Binsbergen, Wim van. *Reconciliation: A Major African Social Technology of Shared and Recognized Humanity (Ubuntu).* Rotterdam: Erasmus University Press, 2001.

Blackman, Rachel. *Partnering with the Local Church.* Teddington: Tearfund, 2007.

Blaikie, Norman. *Designing Social Research: The Logic of Anticipation.* Cambridge: Polity, 2000.

Blennrberger, Erik, and Titti Fränkel. *Ethics in Social Work: An Ethical Code for Social Work Professionals.* Stockholm: Akademikerförbundet SSR, 2006.

Borg, Walter R., et al. *Applying Educational Research: A Practical Guide.* 3rd ed. New York: Longman, 1993.

Bosch, David. *Transforming Mission: Paradigm Shifts in Theology of Mission.* Maryknoll, NY: Orbis, 1991.

Botes, A. C. "A Functional Approach in Nursing Research." *Curationis* 14 (1991) 87–101.

Bourgeois, Donald J. *The Law of Charitable and Not-for-Profit Organizations.* New York: Butterworths, 2002.

Bowles, Wendy, et al. *Ethical Practice in Social Work: An Applied Approach.* Crow's Nest: Allen and Unwin, 2006.

Bowman, Woods. "Should Donors Care About Overhead Costs? Do They Care?" *Nonprofit and Voluntary Sector Quarterly* 35 (2006) 288–310.

Bright, Susan. "Charity and Trusts for the Public Benefit: Time for a Rethink?" *Conveyance* 28 (1989) 36–37.

Bromley, Blake. "1601 Preamble: The State's Agenda for Charity." *Charity Law and Practice Review* 17 (2002) 50–78.

Broodryk, Johann. *Ubuntu: Life Lessons from Africa.* Pretoria: National Library, 2002.

———. *Ubuntu: Life Lesson from Africa.* Pretoria: Ubuntu School of Philosophy, 2004

Browning, Don S. *A Fundamental Practical Theology: Descriptive and Strategic Proposals.* Minneapolis: Fortress, 1991.

Brundage, Anthony. *The English Poor Laws.* New York: Palgrave, 2002.

# Bibliography

Bryant, Antony, and Kathy Charmaz, eds. *The SAGE Handbook of Grounded Theory*. London: SAGE, 2008.

Bullis, Ronald K. *Spirituality in Social Work Practice*. Washington: Taylor and Francis, 1996.

Burger, Ronelle, and Dineo Seabe. "NGO Accountability in Africa." In *The Handbook of Civil Society in Africa*, edited by Ebenezer Obadare, 77–91. Nonprofit and Civil Society Studies 20. New York, NY: Springer, 2014.

Burgess-Van Aken, Barbara. "Goals of Philanthropy." *FSSO 119-100 Controversies in Philanthropy*, November 22, 2021. https://scalar.case.edu/fsso-119-philanthropy-/media/goals-of-philanthropy.

Burns, Nancy, and Susan Grove. *The Practice of Nursing Research: Appraisal, Synthesis, and Generation of Evidence*. 6th ed. St. Louis, MO: Saunders Elsevier, 2009.

Cambridge English Dictionary (CED). "Donor." *Cambridge English Dictionary*, 2024. https://dictionary.cambridge.org/dictionary/english/donor.

Canda, Edward, and Leola Furman. *Spiritual Diversity in Social Work Practice: The Heart of Helping*. New York: Free Press, 1999.

Candid. "What Is an Ngo? What Role Does It Play in Civil Society?" https://grantspace.org/resources/knowledge-base/ngo-definition-and-role.

Carneades.org. "What is Ubuntu Philosophy? (African Philosophy)." April 28, 2019. https://www.youtube.com/watch?v=E_naFb_kdCQ.

Carrington, Ann M. "An Integrated Spiritual Practice Framework for Use Within Social Work." *Journal of Religion & Spirituality in Social Work* 32.4 (2013) 287–312.

Central Statistical Office (CSO), Zambia. *2010 Census of Population and Housing*. Population Summary Report. Lusaka: Central Statistical Office, 2012

———. *2015 Living Conditions Monitoring Survey Report*. Lusaka: Central Statistical Office, 2016.

Charmaz, Kathy. "Grounded Theory in the Twenty-First Century: Applications for Advancing Social Justice Studies." In *The SAGE Handbook of Qualitative Research*, edited by Norman K. Denzin, 507–35. 3rd ed. Thousand Oaks: SAGE, 2005.

Chen, James. "Common Law: What It Is, How It's Used, and How It Differs From Civil Law." *Investopedia*, February 12, 2024. https://www.investopedia.com/terms/c/common-law.asp.

Chesterman, Michael R. "Charities, Trusts and Social Welfare." *Weidenfeld and Nicolson* 16 (1979) 24–28.

Chinn, Peggy, and Maeona Kramer. *Theory and Nursing: A Systematic Approach*. 4th ed. St. Louis, MO: Mosby, 1995.

CohenMiller, Anna S. "How Would You Define a 'Model' within a Theoretical Research?" *Researchgate.net*, January 28, 2015. https://www.researchgate.net/post/how-would-you-define-a-model-within-a-theoretical-research.

Collier, Paul. *The Bottom Billion: Why the Poorest Countries are Failing and What Can Be Done About It*. Oxford: Oxford University Press, 2007.

Collins, John N. *Diakonia: Re-Interpreting the Ancient Sources*. New York: Oxford University Press, 1990.

Congress, Elaine. *Social Work Values and Ethics: Identifying and Resolving Professional Dilemmas*. Chicago: Nelson-Hall, 1999.

———. "What Social Workers Should Know About Ethics: Understanding and Resolving Ethical Dilemmas." *Advances in Social Work* 1 (2000) 1–25.

# Bibliography

Coughlan, Michael, et al. "Step-By-Step Guide to Critiquing Research. Part 1: Quantitative Research." *Br J Nurs* 16.11 (2007) 658–63.

Creswell, John W. *Research Design: Qualitative, Quantitative, and Mixed Method Approaches.* 2nd ed. Thousand Oaks: SAGE, 2003.

———. *Research Design: Qualitative, Quantitative, and Mixed Methods Approaches.* 4th ed. Thousand Oaks: SAGE, 2014.

Cunningham, Katie, and Marc Ricks. "Why Measure?" *Stanford Social Innovation Review* 2 (2004) 44–51.

Dal Pont, Gino. "Why Define Charity? Is the Search for Meaning Worth the Effort?" *Third Sector Review* 8 (2002) 5–37.

Delport, Christa S. L., and Christa B. Fouché. "The Place of Theory and the Literature Review in Qualitative Approach to Research." In *Research at Grassroots: For the Social Sciences and Human Service Professions*, edited by C. B. Fouché, 265–69. 3rd ed. Pretoria: Van Schaik, 2005.

Dickoff, James, et al. "Theory in a Practice Discipline: Part 1. Practice Oriented Theory." *Nursing Research* 17.5 (1968) 415–35.

Dolgoff, Ralf, et al. *Ethical Decisions for Social Work Practice.* 9th ed. Belmont: Brooks Cole, 2012.

Dorey, Pete. *The Sage Encyclopedia of World Poverty: Charity Organization Society.* Thousand Oaks: Sage, 2015.

Douglas, James D., and Tenney, Merrill C., eds. *The New International Dictionary of the Bible.* Grand Rapids: Zondervan, 1987.

Ebimgbo, Samuel O., et al. *Spirituality and Religion in Social Work.* Nsukka: University of Nigeria, 2019.

Engelke, Ernst. *Die Wissenschaft Soziale Arbeit: Werdegang und Grundlagen.* Feiburg: Lambertus, 2004.

Erikson, Erik H. *Identity: Youth and Crisis.* New York: Norton, 1968.

Erikson, Kai. "A Comment to Disguised Observation in Psychology." *Social Problems* 14 (1967) 366–73.

European Symposium on Spirituality, Ethics, and Social Work. "Spirituality in Social Work." https://eventos.ucam.edu/60656/detail/european-symposion-on-spirituality-ethics-and-social-work.html.

Gehrig, Rainer B., et al., eds. "Spirituality in Social Work." *European Symposium on Spirituality, Ethics, and Social Work*, February 26, 2021. https://eventos.ucam.edu/60656/detail/european-symposion-on-spirituality-ethics-and-social-work.html.

Evans, Etresia M. "A Theological Perspective on the Holistic Needs of Emeritus Pastors of the Apostolic Faith Mission of SA." PhD diss., North-West University, Potchefstroom, South Africa, 2014.

Fishman, James J. "The Political Use of Private Benevolence: The Statute of Charitable Uses." *Elisabeth Haub School of Law Faculty Publications* 487 (2008). https://digitalcommons.pace.edu/lawfaculty/487.

Fowler, James. *Stages of Faith.* San Francisco: Harper & Row, 1981.

Gabriel, Tom. *The Human Factor in Rural Development.* London: Belhaven, 1991.

Garcia-Irons, Alexis N. *The Place of Spirituality in Social Work: Practitioners' Personal Views and Beliefs.* San Bernardino: California State University, 2018.

Gautier, Arthur. "Building a Philanthropic Strategy." *ESSEC*, February 14, 2020. https://knowledge.essec.edu/en/society/building-philanthropic-strategy.html.

# Bibliography

Gibson, William J., and Andrew Brown. *Working with Qualitative Data*. London: Sage, 2009.

Glatter, Kathryn A., and Paul Finkelman. "History of the Plague: An Ancient Pandemic for the Age of Covid-19." *American Journal of Medicine* 134 (2021) 176–81. https://doi.org/10.1016/j.amjmed.2020.08.019.

Gomez, Manuel A. *Introduction to Ethics*. El Paso, TX: El Paso Community College, 2023.

Goodrick, Edward W., and John R. Kohlenberger III. *The NIV Exhaustive Concordance*. Grand Rapids: Zondervan, 1999.

Gousmett, Michael. *Modernizing Charity Law: An Overview of the Main Policies Used to Encourage Philanthropy in New Zealand*. Christchurch: University of Canterbury, 2009.

Gravells, Nigel P. "Public Purpose Trusts." *Modern Law Review* 40 (1977) 377–504.

Gray, Mel. "Viewing Spirituality in Social Work through the Lens of Contemporary Social Theory." *British Journal of Social Work* 38 (2008) 175–96.

Gripper, Ruth, and Lona Joy. *What Makes a Good Charity? NPC's Guide to Charity Analysis*. London: New Philanthropy Capital, 2016.

Guion, Lisa A. *Triangulation: Establishing the Validity of Qualitative Studies*. Gainesville: University of Florida, 2002.

Hale, Thomas. *The Applied New Testament Commentary*. Eastbourne: Kingsway, 2000.

Halsbury, L. C., et al. *Commissioners for Special Purposes of Income Tax v. Pemsel: Between Commissioners for Special Purposes of Income Tax—Appellants and John Fredrick Pemsel—Respondent*. London: House of Lords, 1891. https://www.parliament.wa.gov.au/publications/tabledpapers.nsf/displaypaper/3912668a6ae5511fce7ec38e48257df8003568fc/$file/2668.pdf.

Harding, Matthew, et al. *Defining Charity: A Literature Review*. Melbourne: Melbourne Law School, 2011.

Hardt, Jochen, et al. "The Spirituality Questionnaire: Core Dimensions of Spirituality." *Psychology* 3.1 (2012) 116–22.

Harrington, Austin, ed. *Modern Social Theory: An Introduction*. Oxford: Oxford University Press, 2005.

Harvey, Lee. "Social Research Glossary." *Quality Research International*, January 8, 2024. https://www.qualityresearchinternational.com/socialresearch/operationalisation.htm.

Hasnan, Suhaily, et al. *Issues, Challenges, and the Way Forward for Charitable Organisations in Malaysia*. Shah Alam: Universiti Teknologi MARA, 2012.

Herman, Barbara. "Murder and Mayhem: Violence and Kantian Casuistry." *Monist* 72 (1989) 411–32.

———. "Mutual Aid and Respect for Persons." *Ethics* 94 (1984) 577–602.

Hill, Thomas E., ed. *The Blackwell Guide to Kant's Ethics*. West Sussex: Blackwell, 2009.

———. "Duties and Choices in Philanthropic Giving." In *The Ethics of Giving: Philosophers' Perspectives on Philanthropy*, edited by Paul Woodruff, 13–39. Kindle ed. Oxford: Oxford University Press, 2018.

Hoek, Edgar van, and Sue Yardley. *Keeping Communities Clean: The Church's Response to Improving Sanitation and Hygiene*. Teddington: Tearfund, 2009.

Holden, Andrew. *Jehovah's Witnesses: Portrait of a Contemporary Religious Movement*. London: Routledge, 2000.

Holliday, Adrian. *Doing and Writing Qualitative Research*. 2nd ed. London: SAGE, 2010.

*Holy Bible: Revised Standard Version*. Nairobi: Bible Society of Kenya, 2008.

# Bibliography

Hoogen, Toine van den. "Spirituality in the Perspective of Foundational Theology." *HTS Teologiese Studies/Theological Studies* 70 (2014) 1–6.

Hoque, Zahirul, and Lee Parker. *Performance Management in Nonprofit Organisations: Global Perspectives.* London: Routledge, 2015.

Hugman, Richard. "Social Work Research and Ethics." In *The SAGE Handbook of Social Work Research*, edited by Ian J. Shaw, 149–63. Los Angeles: SAGE, 2010.

Ife, Jim. "Realising the Purpose of Social Work for Stakeholders: Maintaining the Vision and Making a Difference in a World of Change." In vol. 1 of *25th AASW National Conference: Social Work Influencing Outcomes*, 16–26. Canberra: Australian Association of Social Workers, 1997.

Initiative for Climate Action Transparency (ICAT). *Sustainable Development Methodology: Assessing the Environmental, Social, and Economic Impacts of Policies and Actions.* Edited by D. Rich et al. Washington, DC: World Resources Institute, 2020. https://climateactiontransparency.org/icat-toolbox/sustainable-development.

Institute of Chartered Accountants of India (ICAI). *A Study on Laws Governing Charitable Organisations in India.* New Delhi: Committee for Cooperatives and NPO Sectors, 2014.

International Federation of Social Work (IFSW). "Global Definition of Social Work." July 2014. http://ifsw.org/get-involved/global-definition-of-social-work.

Iwaarden, Jos van, et al. "Charities: How Important Is Performance to Donors?" *International Journal of Quality & Reliability Management* 26 (2014) 5–22.

Jeppe, Wilhelm J. O. *Community Development: An African Rural Approach.* Pretoria: Africa Institute, 1985.

Jovago, Josephine Wawira. "Whatever Happened to the Spirit of Ubuntu?" *Lusaka Times*, May 8, 2016. https://www.lusakatimes.com/2016/05/08/whatever-happened-spirit-ubuntu.

Kamwangamalu, Nkonko M. "Ubuntu in South Africa: A Sociolinguistic Perspective to a Pan-African Concept." *Journal of Critical Arts* 13 (1999) 24–42.

Kang'ethe, Simon, and Tatenda Manomano. "Exploring the Challenges Threatening the Survival of NGOs in Selected African Countries." *Mediterranean Journal of Social Sciences* 5 (2014) 1495–1500.

Kaniaru, Donald, et al. *Capacity Building for Sustainable Development: An Overview of UNEP Environmental Capacity Development Initiatives.* Nairobi: UNEP, 2002. https://www.unep.org/resources/report/capacity-building-sustainable-development-overview-unep-environmental-capacity.

Kant, Immanuel. *Prolegomena to Any Future Metaphysics.* London: Macmillan, 1783.

Kaptein, Muel, and Johan Wempe. "Three General Theories of Ethics and the Integrative Role of the Integrity Approach." *SSRN*, October 7, 2011. https://ssrn.com/abstract=1940393.

Katz, Michale B. *The Undeserving Poor.* 2nd ed. New York: Oxford University Press, 2013.

Kgatla, Salaelo T. "Relationships Are Building Blocks to Social Justice: Cases of Biblical Justice and African Ubuntu." *HTS Theological Studies* 72.1 (2016). https://hts.org.za/index.php/hts/article/view/3239/8572.

King, Ursula. *The Search for Spirituality: Our Global Quest for a Spiritual Life.* Norwich: Canterbury, 2009.

Kirmayer, Laurence J., et al., eds. *The Mental Health of Indigenous Peoples.* Culture and Mental Health Research Unit Report 10. Montreal: Institute of Community and Family Psychiatry, 2005.

# Bibliography

Knight, Shirlee-Ann, et al. "The Context and Contextual Constructs of Research." Paper presented at Fifth Conference on Qualitative Research in IT: The Context and Contextual Constructs of Research, November 29–30, 2010, Brisbane, Australia. https://www.researchgate.net/publication/224932425_The_Context_and_Contextual_Constructs_of_Research.

Koenig, Harold G., and David Larson. "Religion and Mental Health: Evidence for an Association." *International Review of Psychiatry* 13 (2001) 67–78.

Korac-Kakabadse, Nada, et al. "Spirituality and Leadership Praxis." *Journal of Managerial Psychology* 17 (2002) 165–82.

Kritzinger, J. J. *Navorsing in die Fakulteit Teologie: Riglyne vir Studente*. Pretoria: Universiteit van Pretoria, 2000.

Kuhn, Wagner. *The Need for a Biblical Theology of Holistic Mission*. Faculty Publications 12. Berrein Springs: Andrews University, 2005.

Latvus, Kari. *Diaconia as Care for the Poor: Critical Perspectives on the Development of Caritative Diaconia*. Hammareninkatu: Kirkon tutkimuskeskuksen verkkojulkaisuja, 2017.

Lechterman, Ted. "An Ethical Guide to Responsible Giving." *Conversation*, November 28, 2017. http://theconversation.com/an-ethical-guide-to-responsible-giving-87984.

Lezotte, Edna. "Spirituality and Social Work." December 2010. https://cdn.ymaws.com/www.naswma.org/resource/resmgr/imported/fce_spiritualityandsocialwork.pdf

Lincoln, Yvonna S., and Egon G. Guba. *Naturalistic Inquiry*. London: Sage, 1985.

Loue, Sana. *Social Work Values, Ethics, and Spirituality. Handbook of Religion and Spirituality in Social Work Practice and Research*. New York: Springer-Verlag, 2017.

Louw, Daniel. *Interculturality and Wholeness in African Spiritualities and Cosmologies: The Need for Communality (Ubuntu—Philosophy) and Compassionate Co-Humanity (Utugi–Hospitality) in the Realm of Pastoral Caregiving*. Stellenbosch: Stellenbosch University, 2014.

Louw, Johannes P., and Eugene A. Nida. *Indices*. Vol. 2 of *Greek-English Lexicon of the New Testament Based on Semantic Domains*. New York: United Bible Societies, 1988.

Mabvurira, Vincent. "Hunhu/Ubuntu Philosophy as a Guide for Ethical Decision Making in Social Work." *African Journal of Social Work* 10 (2020) 74–77.

Magnus, George. *The Age of Aging: How Demographics Are Changing the Global Economy and Our World*. Singapore: Wiley & Sons, 2009.

Mahrik, Tibor. "The End Justifies the Means—Ethical Analysis." *Edukacja Etyczna*, January 2018. DOI:10.24917/20838972.14.8.

Malik, Nuzhat. "Defining 'Charity' and 'Charitable Purposes' in the United Kingdom." *International Journal of Not-for-Profit Law* 11.1 (2008). https://www.icnl.org/resources/research/ijnl/defining-charity-and-charitable-purposes-in-the-united-kingdom.

Malinga, Tumani, et al. "Ethical Dilemmas in Social Work Practice: Case of Botswana." In *Ethical Issues in Social Work Practice*, edited by Ana Frunză amd Antonio Sandu, 82–104. Hershey, PA: IGI Global, 2018.

Mandela, Nelson R. *Long Walk to Freedom: The Autobiography of Nelson Mandela*. New York: Hachette, 1994.

Manfred-Gilham, Jerry J. "An Experiential Approach to Teaching the Integration of Spirituality and Social Work." Paper presented at NACSW's 59th Annual Convention and Training Conference, Indianapolis, IN, October 29–November 1, 2009.

# BIBLIOGRAPHY

Manpower Development Corp. (MDC). *The Alleghany Foundation: Strategic Thinking for Community Transformation*. Chapel Hill: MDC, 2011.

Manser, Martin H. *The New Matthew Henry Commentary: The Classical Work with Updated Language*. Grand Rapids: Zondervan, 2010.

Marshall, Catherine, and Gretchen B. Rossman. *Designing Qualitative Research*. 4th ed. Thousand Oaks: SAGE, 2006.

Martin, Fiona. "The Legal Concept of Charity and Its Expansion After the Aid/Watch Decision." *Cosmopolitan Civil Societies Journal* 3 (2011) 20–33.

Mbiti, John. *African Religions and Philosophy*. New Hampshire: Heinemann, 1990.

McGregor-Lowndes, Myles. "Diversions of Charitable Assets: Crimes and Punishments in Australia." Paper presented at the 16th Annual Conference of the National Centre on Philanthropy and the Law: Reforming the Charitable Contribution Deduction, New York, 2004.

Metz, Thaddeus. "The African Ethic of Ubuntu." *1000-Word Philosophy* (blog), September 8, 2019. https://1000wordphilosophy.com/2019/09/08/the-african-ethic-of-ubuntu.

Ministry of Community Development and Social Services (MCDSS), Zambia. *National Policy on Non-Governmental Organisations: A Coordinated NGO Sector for Citizens' Wellbeing*. Lusaka: MCDSS, 2018.

———. *NGO File 2018*. Mongu: MCDSS, 2018.

———. *NGO Act 2009*. Lusaka: MCDSS, 2009.

Ministry of Tourism (MT), Zambia. *Application for Inscription of Barotse Plains on the World Heritage Site*. Lusaka: National Heritage Conservation Commission, 2021.

Mokgoro, Yvonne. "Ubuntu and the Law in South Africa." *Buffalo Human Rights Law Review* 4 (1998) 15–23. https://digitalcommons.law.buffalo.edu/bhrlr/vol4/iss1/3.

Moss, Bernard. "Spirituality and Social Care: Contributing to Personal and Community Wellbeing." *The British Journal of Social Work* 33 (2003) 578–80.

Mouton, Johann. *Understanding Social Research*. Pretoria: Van Schaik, 1996.

Mungai, Ndungi. "Afrocentric Social Work: Implications for Practice Issues." In *Some Aspects of Community Empowerment and Resilience*, edited by Bharath Bhushan Mamidi and Venkat Rao Pulla, 63–76. New Delhi: Allied, 2015.

Murphy, Nancey. *Reasoning and Rhetoric in Religion*. Valley Forge, PA: Trinity, 1994.

Mutemwa, David. "The Effectiveness of Sesheke Church's Transformational Task: A Practical Theological Perspective." MA thesis, North-West University, Potchefstroom, South Africa, 2017.

———. "A Practical Theological Model for a Community Transformation Strategy Implemented by the Church in Sesheke." PhD diss., North-West University, Potchefstroom, South Africa, 2021.

Muyingi, Mbangu. "African Ethics and the Moral Possibilities of Ubuntu towards Conflict Resolution in the Democratic Republic of Congo." *Mediterranean Journal of Social Sciences* 4 (2013) 561–68.

Mweene, Confucious. "An Assessment of Community Participation and Empowerment Through Non Governmental Organizations' Development Work Among the Rural Poor." MA Thesis, Norwegian University of Science and Technology, 2006.

Natter, Raymond. "Do the Ends Justify the Means." *Our Perspectives*, June 2014. https://snwlawfirm.com/wp-content/uploads/2020/12/2014-06-Natter.pdf.

Neagoe, Alexandru. "Ethical Dilemmas of the Social Work Professional in a (Post) Secular Society: With Special Reference to the Christian Social Worker." *International Social Work* 56 (2013) 310–25.

# Bibliography

Nexus Marketing. "Types of Charities." *Top Nonprofits* (blog), n.d. https://topnonprofits.com/lists/types-of-charities.

Niekerk, Brimadevi van. "Spirituality and Religion: What Are the Fundamental Differences?" *HTS Teologiese Studies/Theological Studies* 74 (2018) 1–11.

Ngaira, Josephine Khaoma W. "Impact of Climate Change on Agriculture in Africa by 2030." *Scientific Research and Essays* 2 (2007) 238–43.

Ng'weshemi, Andrea M. *Rediscovering the Human: The Quest for a Christo-Theological Anthropology in Africa*. New York: Peter Lang, 2002.

Nightingale, Andrea Joslyn. *Triangulation*. Oslo: University of Oslo, 2020.

Nmah, Patrick. "Christian Fundamentalism in Nigeria: A Pluralistic Moral Maxim." *Journal of Contemporary Research* 8 (2011) 321–337.

Noller, Annette. "Church in the Mission of Jesus Christ: Diaconal Action Between Congregation, Community, and Social Enterprises." *Caritas et Veritas* 9 (2019) 49–57.

Nordquist, Richard. "Premises and Conclusions: Definitions and Examples in Arguments." *ThoughtCo.*, September 12, 2024. thoughtco.com/premise-argument-1691662.

Nordstokke, Kjell, ed. *Diakonia in Context: Transformation, Reconciliation, Empowerment*. Geneva: Lutheran World Federation, 2009.

———. "The Study of Diakonia as an Academic Discipline." In *Diakonia as Christian Social Practice: An Introduction*, edited by Stephanie Dietrich et al., 46–61. Oxford: Regnum, 2014.

Obiagwu, Obinna, and Jude Onuoha. "The Implication of Kant's Moral Philosophy in Our Society Today." *Journal of Philosophy and Ethics* 1 (2019) 30–38.

Okwokwo, Believe. "Social Work in a Global Context." *LinkedIn*, March 13, 2023. https://www.linkedin.com/pulse/social-work-global-context-believe-okwokwo.

Opatrný, Michal. "Caritas Theory as Theological Discourse within Education in Social Work." *Journal of Religion & Spirituality in Social Work* 39 (2020) 299–323.

Oppenheim, Claire. "Nelson Mandela and the Power of Ubuntu." *Religions* 2 (2012) 369–88.

Osakwe, Patrick N., and Miriam Poretti. *Trade and Poverty Alleviation in Africa: The Role of Inclusive Structural Transformation*. Trade and Poverty 2. New York: UNCTAD, 2015

Osmer, Richard R. *Practical Theology: An Introduction*. Grand Rapids: Eerdmans, 2008.

Owoye, Oluwole, and Nicole Bissessar. "Bad Governance and Corruption in Africa: Symptoms of Leadership and Institutional Failure." *Journal of Applied Professional Studies* 2.4 (2021). https://www.journal-aps.net/issue-4.

Oxford Review. "Phronesis: Definition and Meaning." *Oxford Review Encyclopaedia of Terms*, January 2024. https://www.oxford-review.com/oxford-review-encyclopaedia-terms/phronesis-definition-meaning.

Oxhandler, Holly, and Danielle Parrish. "Integrating Clients' Religion/Spirituality in Clinical Practice: A Comparison Among Social Workers, Psychologists, Counselors, Marriage and Family Therapists, and Nurses." *Journal of Clinical Psychology* 74 (2018) 680–94.

Patton, Michael Q. *Qualitative Research and Evaluation Methods*. 3rd ed. Thousand Oaks: Sage, 2002.

Parse, Rosemarie Rizzo, et al. "Nursing Research: Qualitative and Methodological Comparisons with the Qualitative Approach." *Journal of College Student Development* 32 (1985) 389–97.

# BIBLIOGRAPHY

Payne, Malcolm. *Modern Social Work Theory*. London: Macmillan Education, 2014.

Pender, John, et al. "Strategies for Sustainable Development in the Ethiopian Highlands." *American Journal of Agricultural Economics* 83 (2001) 1231–40.

Placenza, Giorgio. "Interview with Roy Bhaskar." Integral Theory Conference, July 2013, San Francisco, CA. Video. http://www.youtube.com/watch?v=8YGHZPg-19k.

Popple, Philip R., and Leslie Leighninger. *Social Work, Social Welfare & American Society*. 8th ed. Boston: Allyn and Bacon, 2011.

Proirier, Donald. *Charity Law in New Zealand*. Wellington: Department of Internal Affairs, New Zealand, 2013. https://www.charities.govt.nz/assets/uploads/resources/charity-law-in-new-zealand.pdf.

Radovanović, Bojana. "Kant's Moral Theory as a Guide in Philanthropy." *Philosophy and Society* 33 (2022) 585–600.

Reamer, Frederic. "Ethical Theories and Social Work Practice." In *The Routledge Handbook of Social Work Ethics and Values*, edited by Stephen Marson and Robert McKinney, 15–21. London: Routledge, 2019.

———. *Social Work Values and Ethics*. 3rd ed. New York: Columbia University Press, 2006.

Richardson, Frank, and Blaine J. Fowers. "Interpretive Social Science: An Overview." *American Behavioral Scientist* 41 (1998) 465–95.

Ricoeur, Paul. *Oneself as Another*. Chicago: University of Chicago Press, 1992.

Rosenblatt, Louise M. "The Transactional Model of Reading and Writing." In *Theoretical Models and Processes of Reading*, edited by Robert B. Ruddell et al., 1363–98. Newark, DE: IRA.

Russell, Cynthia. "Evaluating Quantitative Research Reports." *Nephrology Nursing Journal* 32 (2005) 61–64.

Samuel, Vinay, and Chris Sugden, eds. *Mission as Transformation*. Oxford: Regnum, 1999.

Sandelowski, Margarete. "What Is in a Name? Qualitative Description Revisited." *Res Nurs Health* 33 (2010) 77–84.

Sandle, Genevieve. "What Is Kantian Ethics?" *Perlego*, March 6, 2023. https://www.perlego.com/knowledge/study-guides/what-is-kantian-ethics.

Sapsford, Roger, and Victor Jupp. *Data Collection and Analysis*. 2nd ed. London: SAGE, 2006.

Schmidt, Jeff. "Kantian Ethics." *Corporate Finance Institute (CFI)*, n.d. https://corporatefinanceinstitute.com/resources/esg/kantian-ethics.

Schurink, Emma M. "Deciding to Use a Qualitative Research Approach." In *Research at Grassroots: A Primer for the Caring Professions*, edited by A. S. de Vos, 239–51. Pretoria: Van Schaik, 1998.

Schwandt, Thomas A. *Qualitative Inquiry: A Dictionary of Terms*. Thousand Oaks: SAGE, 2001.

Seale, Clive, et al., eds. *Qualitative Research Practice*. London: SAGE, 2010.

Seinfeld, Jeffrey. "Spirituality in Social Work Practice." *Clinical Social Work Journal* 40 (2012) 240–44.

Seixas, Brayan, et al. "The Qualitative Descriptive Approach in International Comparative Studies: Using Online Qualitative Surveys." *International Journal of Health Policy Management* 7 (2018) 778–81.

Shapcott, Richard. "Phronesis, Ethics, and Realism." *E-International Relations*, February 7, 2013. https://www.e-ir.info/2013/02/07/phronesis-ethics-and-realism.

# BIBLIOGRAPHY

Shava, Elvin. "Accountability of Non-Governmental Organisations in Poverty Alleviation Programmes." *Africa Insight* 49 (2019) 122–36.

Sher, Gila. "Lessons on Truth from Kant." *Analytic Philosophy* 58 (2017) 171–201.

Sheridan, Michael, et al. "Practitioners' Personal and Professional Attitudes and Behaviors Toward Religion and Spirituality: Issues for Education and Practice." *Journal of Social Work Education* 28 (2014) 190–203.

Sheridan, M. J., and Anne J. Kisor. "The Research Process and the Elderly." In *Gerontological Social Work: Knowledge, Service, Settings, and Special Populations*, edited by Robert L. Schneider, 96–135. 2nd ed. Boston: Brooks/Cole Thomson Learning, 2000.

Shutte, Augustine. *Ubuntu: An Ethics for a New South Africa*. Pietermaritzburg: Luster. 2001.

Silverman, David. *Doing Qualitative Research*. 2nd ed. London: SAGE, 2006.

Šimr, Karel. "Diakonia in the Public Sphere—A Daughter of the Church, or Its Sister? Church and Diakonia between Separation and Approximation." *Caritas et Veritas* 7 (2017) 154–60.

Solomon, Robert. *Spiritualiteit Voor Sceptici*. Amsterdam: Ten Have, 2002.

Speth, Gus. "Living on Earth: Protecting our Environmental Resources and Promoting Social Justice." *WineWaterWatch*, May 5, 2016. http://winewaterwatch.org/2016/05/we-scientists-dont-know-how-to-do-that-what-a-commentary.

Šrajer, Jindřich. "Etika a Požadavek Komplexnosti v Pociální Práci." *Sociální Práce/Sociálná Práca* 12 (2012) 81–88.

Stebbins, Robert A. *Exploratory Research in the Social Sciences: What Is Exploration?* Thousand Oaks: SAGE, 2011.

Stetzar, Ed, and David Putman. *Breaking the Missional Code*. Nashville: Broadman and Holman, 2006.

Sticker, Martin. "True Need in Kant." *De Gruyter* 11 (2022) 432–58.

Struwig, F. W., and G.B. Stead. *Planning, Designing, and Reporting Research*. Cape Town: Pearson Education South Africa, 2001.

Swanepoel, Hennie, and Frik de Beer. *Community Development: Breaking the Cycle of Poverty*. 5th ed. Lansdowne: Juta, 2015.

Swarbrick, David. "Income Tax Special Commissioners v Pemsel: HL 20 Jul 1891. Charitable Purposes Used with Technical Meaning." *Swarb.co.uk* (blog), August 24, 2021. https://swarb.co.uk/income-tax-special-commissioners-v-pemsel-hl-20-jul-1891.

Swedberg, Richard. *On the Uses of Exploratory Research and Exploratory Studies in Social Sciences*. New York: Cornell University, 2018.

Tacey, David. *The Spirituality Revolution: The Emergence of Contemporary Spirituality*. London: Routledge, 2004.

Talbot, Laura T. *Principles and Practice of Nursing Research*. St. Louis, MO: Mosby, 1994.

Tesoriero, Frank. *Community Development: Community-Based Alternatives in an Age of Globalization*. Frenchs Forest, NSW: Pearson, 2010.

Thompson, Mel. *Understanding Ethics*. 5th ed. London: Hodder Education, 2010.

———. *Understanding Political Philosophy*. 2nd ed. London: Hodder Education, 2010.

Thorne, Sally. "Ethical and Representational Issues in Qualitative Secondary Analysis." *Qualitative Health Research* 8 (1998) 547–54.

Tirkey, Christopher A. B. *An Outline of Spirituality*. New Delhi: Indian Society for Promoting Christian Knowledge, 2006.

# Bibliography

Touré-Tillery, Maferima, and Ayelet Fishbach. "The End Justifies the Means, But Only in the Middle." *Journal of Experimental Psychology: General* 141 (2011) 570–83.

Training and Resources in Research Ethics Evaluation (TRREE). *Introduction to Research Ethics*. Module 1. Pok Fu Lam, Hong Kong: University of Hong Kong, 2014. http://elearning.trree.org.

Treasury, Australia. *A Definition of Charity*. Canberra: Commonwealth of Australia, 2011.

Tutu, Desmond. *God Has a Dream: A Vision of Hope for Our Time*. New York: Doubleday, 2004.

United Nations Department of Economic and Social Affairs (UNDESA). "Youth Education, Employment, and Empowerment Key to Global Progress." https://www.un.org/development/desa/youth/youth-education-employment-and-empowerment-key-to-global-progress.html.

United Nations Division for Sustainable Development Goals (UNDSDG). "The Seventeen Goals." https://sdgs.un.org/goals.

University of Exeter. "Human Societies Evolve Along Similar Paths." *Phys.org*, December 18, 2017. https://phys.org/news/2017-12-human-societies-evolve-similar-paths.html.

Unrepresented Nations and Peoples Organization (UNPO). "Self-Determination." *Unpo.org*, September 21, 2017. https://old.unpo.org/article/4957.

Vilani, Daniela, et al. "The Role of Spirituality and Religiosity in Subjective Well-Being of Individuals with Different Religious Status." *Frontiers in Psychology* 10 (2019) 1–11.

Villegas, Diana L. "Spirituality and Belief: Implications for Study and Practice of Christian Spirituality." *HTS Teologiese Studies/Theological Studies* 74(2018) 1–8.

Villiers, Peter G. R. de. "Spirituality, Theology, and the Critical Mind." *Acta Theologica* 27 (2007) 99–121.

Vodo, Teuta. *Faith-Based Organisations: The Role of Christian Organisations to Social Cohesion in EU Member States*. Amersfoort: European Christian Political Movement, 2016.

Vorster, Jakobus M. *Ethical Perspectives on Human Rights*. Potchefstroom: Potchefstroom Theological, 2004.

Walla, Alice P. "Kant's Moral Theory and Demandingness." *Ethic Theory Moral Prac* 18.4 (2015) 731–43.

Walker, Lorraine O., and Kay S. Avant. *Strategies for Theory Construction in Nursing*. 3rd ed. Norwalk: Appleton and Lange, 1995.

Warren, Rick. *The Purpose Driven Church: Growth without Compromising Your Message and Mission*. Grand Rapids: Zondervan, 1995.

Wet, Hannah Lindiwe de. *Understanding Transformational Development in World Vision South Africa: Conceptualisation and Operationalization*. The Hague: International Institute of Social Studies, 2011.

Wilson, Holly Skodol. *Introducing Research in Nursing*. 2nd ed. Los Angeles: Addison & Wesley, 1993.

Wyk, Jan H. van, and Nicolaas Vorster. "An Introduction to the Theological Politico-Ethical Thinking of Koos Vorster." *In die Skriflig/In Luce Verbi* 46 (2012) 1–10.

Yahaya, Abubakar M., and Ali Y. Gunduz. "The Importance of Healthy Human Life on Economic Development." *Social Sciences* 7 (2018) 63–67.

Yarbrough, Donald, et al. *The Program Evaluation Standards: A Guide for Evaluators and Evaluation Users*. 3rd ed. Thousand Oaks: SAGE, 2011.

# Index

Accountability, 4, 42, 48–50, 52, 71, 72, 73, 80–81, 99, 106–10
Adeyemo, Tokunboh, 7
Ajibo, Henry, 30, 30–31
Akintola, Owolabi, 4
Akpenpuun, Joyce Rumun, 35
American Sociological Association, 33
Arendt, Hannah, 41
Art and cultural charities, 17
Atan, Ruhaya, 49
Austin, Michael, 102
Avant, Kay, 123

Bamberger, Michael, 58
Banks, Sarah, 38, 39
Barbie, Earl, 61
Barotse Royal Establishment, 17, 18
Benedict XVI (Pope), 12
Beyer, Hermann, 11
Binsbergen, Wim van, 93
Blackman, Rachel, 45–46
Blackman, Sarah, 113
Blaikie, Norman, 60
Blenberger, Erik, 37–38
Borg, Walter, 60, 130
Bowman, Woods, 50
Bromley, Blake, 22
Broodryk, Johann, 90
Brown, Andrew, 57
Browning, Don, 25, 26, 27, 42, 112
Burger, Ronelle, 4
Burns, Nancy, xvi, 62, 66, 118

Canda, Edward, 35

Caritas theory, 10, 11, 19, 26, 84, 94. *See also* Charity, etymology of; *Diakonia*
Carson, Verna, 34–35
Case study, approaches to
 contextual, 61–62
 descriptive, 60–61
 ethical considerations, 62–64
 exploratory, 59–60
Categorical imperative, 84–88, 97
Catholic theology, 10, 19, 29, 31–32, 84, 94, 104
Charitable NGOs. *See* Charitable organizations
Charitable organizations
 addressing needs of the people, 75–78
 as agents, philanthropic strategies, 112, 114, 119
 among African communities, 18–19
 art and culture charities, 17
 charity, etymology of, 9–13
 climate change, 107
 community participation, 109–112
 corruption in, 73–74
 definition of, 13–15
 duplicative efforts, 71–72
 education in, 77, 107
 educational charities, 16
 employment and empowerment, 76, 107
 environment charities, 17
 ethical aspects, philanthropic strategies, 4–8, 83–101, 102–121
 ethical evaluation of, 4–8, 83–101

# Index

(Charitable organizations, continued)
  ethical reflection on, 42–51
  expectations of participants, 80–81, 108–9
  faith-based organizations (FBOs), 16
  government, political influence, 74
  health, 107
  health charities, 16–17
  impact on community, 67–74
  indigenous employees, 68
  international charities, 18, 49
  lack of skills and understanding of, 73
  monitoring and evaluation of, 72–73
  operating strategies of, 4–8
  as operational praxis, 69–75, 107
  operationalization of, 9–20
  overdependence on support, 72
  poor working culture, 68
  poverty, 75–76, 107
  prevalent in African communities, 16–17
  recipients, 6, 13, 71, 111, 114–15, 118, 119
  resources, misappropriation of, 70–71
  social-cultural aspects, 67–69
  strategies of, 79–80, 107–8, 109, 110
  sustainability, 69–70, 113–14
  theoretical interpretation of, 40–42
  transport and communication, 77, 107
  tribalism and, 69
  types of, 15–18
  uncoordinated and insufficient efforts, 74–75
  wildlife conservation charities, 18
  *See also* Philanthropic strategies
Charities Act of 2006 for England and Wales, 23–24, 43
Charity, etymology of, 9–13, 14, 19, 84, 104
Charity law, historical development of, 18–19, 21–24
Charity Organization Society (COS), 51
Chinn, Peggy, 121–23, 132
Climate change, 33, 78, 107, 114

Collier, Paul, 41–42, 45
Collins, John, 10
Commissioners for Special Purposes of Income Tax v Pemsel. *See* Pemsel Case
Common law
  accountability, 48–50
  charity, etymology of, 13, 14, 15, 19, 21–22
  equality and fairness, 44–46
  ethical perspectives, 40–52, 106
  good practice, 50–51
  poor, deserving and undeserving, 46–48
  self-determination, right to, 44–46
  theoretical perspectives, 106
  transparency, 48–50
Communitarian morality, 91–94, 96
Community capacity building, 115
Community education, 140
Community participation, 109, 110, 111, 113, 116, 119, 125, 126–27, 129, 131, 133
Competence, 31, 105
Congress, Elaine, 38–39, 83
Consequentialism. *See* Teleological ethics
Corruption, 73–74, 97, 100
COS. *See* Charity Organization Society (COS)
Coughlan, Michael, 137

Dal Pont, Gino, 14
De Beer, Frik, 5, 45
*Decent Aid* (model)
  aid strategy, 128, 129–30
  assumptions of, 130–32
  community participation, 126–27, 129
  concepts in, 125–28
  criteria of, 123–24, 132–34
  description of, 121–31
  ethical reflection in, 125–26, 129
  evaluation of, 132–34
  explanation, structure of, 128–30
  further research on, 141
  implementation, working group, 120
  limitations of, 139–40

# Index

overview of, 124
purpose of, 125
recommendations for, 140–41
relationship statements, conceptual, 119–21
summary of, 135–36
true needs of the people, 127–28, 129–30
*See also* Philanthropic strategies
Delport, Christa, 21
Department of National Parks and Wildlife, 18
*Diakonia*, 10–11, 13, 19, 26, 84, 94. *See also* Caritas theory; Charity, etymology of
Dickoff, James, 110, 135
Dignity and worth, human person, 27, 31, 43, 67, 81, 86–87, 92–94, 96, 99, 105, 107
Donor trust, 48–50
Donors, ethical decision making, 5, 46
Dorey, Pete, 47
Douglas, James, 11

Ebimgbo, Samulel, 33
Education, 14, 16, 23, 69, 77, 107
Educational charities, 16
Elizabeth I (Queen), 22, 46
Engelke, Ernst, 26
Environment charities, 17–18
Equal regard, 27–28
Equality and fairness, 43–44
ETHIC model, 39
Ethical dilemmas, in social work, 37–40
Ethical guidelines, donating responsibly, 5, 52
Ethical reflection, 2, 26–27, 80–81, 85, 104, 106, 108–10, 112, 113, 134, 140
Ethical theories, evaluation of, 82–101. *See also* Kantian ethics; Ubuntu philosophy
"Ethicality," 7, 112, 114, 138
European Symposium on Spirituality, Ethics, and Social Work, 34
Evans, Etresia, 115

Faith-Based Organizations (FBOs), 16–17, 49
Fishman, James, 24
Fouché, Christa, 21
Fowers, Blaine, 83
Fränkel, Titti, 37–38
Friedrich Wilhelm IV of Prussia (King), 10
Furman, Leola, 35

Gabriel, Tom, 118–19, 128
Garcia-Irons, Alexis, 34, 36
Gibson, William, 57
Golden rule, 27, 92, 95
Good practice, 28, 50–51, 70, 71, 73, 74, 79, 80, 81, 105, 106, 108
Goodrick, Edward, 11, 28
Gousmett, Michael, 15
Gravells, Nigel, 14
Gray, Mel, 36
Gripper, Ruth, 6
Grove, Susan, xvi, 62, 66, 118
Guba, Egon G., 57
Gunduz, Ali, 77–78

Hale, Thomas, 7
Harding, Matthew, 14, 15
Hardt, Jochen, 32
Harrington, Austin, 41
Hasnan, Suhaily, 49, 112
Health, 16–17, 23, 75, 77–78, 107, 110
Health charities, 16–17
Herman, Barbara, 87
Hill, Thomas, 84
Hoek, Edgar van, 114
Hoogen, Toine van den, 32
Human relationships, 31, 105
Humanity as an end, 87, 93, 96, 118

Indigenous employees, 68
Institute of Chartered Accountants of India, 23
Integrity, 31, 40, 63, 73, 80, 105, 107, 109
International Federation of Social Workers, 30
International NGOs, 18, 49
Irons, Alexis Garcia, 10

# Index

Iwaarden, Jos van, 49, 50

Jordan, William Kitchener, 23
Joy, Lona, 6

Kamwangamalu, Nkonko, 91
Kang'ethe, Simon, 3
Kant, Immanuel, 84–88
Kantian ethics, 84–88, 93–99, 129
Kaptein, Muel, 87
Katz, Michael, 46–47
Keeping Girls in School, 16
Kirmayer, Laurence, 6, 44
Kisor, Anne, 61
Koenig, Harold, 35
Kohlenberger, John, 11, 28
Kramer, Maeona, 121–23, 132
Kuhn, Wagner, 25

Larson, David, 35
Latvus, Karl, 10
"Least of these," meaning of, 12
Lechterman, Ted, 5–6, 43, 50
Lezotte, Edna, 31–32, 35
Lincoln, Yvonna S., 57
Louw, Johannes, 12
Love, lack of ethic of, 94–95
Lutheran World Federation, 26

Mabvurira, Vincent, 89, 90, 93–94, 97, 99
Malaysia, 4, 48
Malik, Nuzhat, 14
Mandela, Nelson, 90, 91
Manomano, Tatenda, 3
Martin, Fiona, 23, 47, 48
Mbiti, John, 92, 98
Member checking (respondent validation), 82, 132
Merriam, Sharan, 59
Ministry of Community Development and Social Services, 2, 63
Model. *See Decent Aid* (model)
Mongu district, ix–xi, xv–xvi, 1–5, 7, 53–64, 65, 67–81, 94–101, 141. *See also* Zambia
Mouton, Johann, 60, 61
Mungai, Ndungi, 93, 99

Muyingi, Mbangu, 92, 93

National Heritage Conservation Commission, 17
NGOs. *See* Non-Governmental Organizations
Ng'weshemi, Andrea, 91
Nida, Eugene, 12
Nigeria, 4
Nmah, Patrick, 35
Noller, Annette, 13
Non-Governmental Organizations (NGOs), xv–xvi, 1–8, 68–73, 79–80, 97, 98, 99, 107–9, 117–18, 120, 138
Non-profit organizations (NPOs), 18, 49
Nordstokke, Kjell, 26

Obiagwu, Obinna, 85
Okwokwo, Believe, 88
Onuoha, Jude, 85
Opatrný, Michal, 26, 88, 115
Operationalization, charitable organizations, 9–20
Oppenheim, Claire, 90
Osmer, Richard, 26–27, 56, 59, 82, 83, 85, 95, 126

Participants, in charitable organizations, 69–75
Pastoral theology, 25–29, 104
Patton, Michael, 59
Payne, Malcolm, 102
Pemsel Case, 14, 15, 17, 19, 43
Philanthropic aid, recipients, 6, 13, 71, 111, 113–15, 118
Philanthropic strategies
  criteria for ethical evaluation, 83–94
  cultural context of, 115–16, 119
  ethical aspects of, 4–8, 83–101, 102–21, 138
  evaluation of ethical aspects, 94–101
  holistic approach, 7, 103, 116–17, 118, 119
  methodology, ethical aspects, 53–64
  model for ethical evaluation, 102–36
  policies and guidelines, 117–19

# Index

techniques, ethical evaluation, 116–17
*See also* Charitable organizations
Phronesis. *See* Practical moral reasoning
Poor, deserving and undeserving, 42, 46–48, 52, 71, 80, 106, 107, 109, 114
Poverty, 14, 23, 45, 47–48, 75–76, 81, 107, 110, 113
Practical moral reasoning (*Phronesis*), 28–29, 39, 40, 74, 83, 100, 104, 107, 108
Preamble to the Statute of Charitable Causes. *See* Statute of Elizabeth of 1601
Proirier, Donald, 22, 24
Protestant theology, 10, 19, 26, 29, 31, 84, 94, 104
Putnam, David, 3

Qualitative inquiry, as research methodology, 59–62
Quantitative inquiry, as research methodology, 55

Radovanović, Bojana, 84, 86, 100
Reamer, Frederic, 38–39, 83
Research methodology
  ethical aspects of, 62–64
  member checking (respondent validation), 82, 132
  qualitative inquiry, 59–62
  strategy for, 55–56
  triangulation, 57–58
Richardson, Frank, 83
Ricoeur, Paul, 26
Rosenblatt, Louise, 121
Russel, Cynthia, 137

SDGs. *see* Sustainable Development Goals (SDGs)
Seabe, Dineo, 4
Self-determination, right to, 37, 42, 44–46, 52, 72, 81, 106, 107, 109, 113
Service, social, 30, 105
Shava, Elvin, 4

Sheridan, Michael, 36, 61
Šimr, Karel, 13
Social justice, 30, 31, 43, 71, 75, 80, 99, 105, 107, 109
Social work
  *Decent Aid* (model), 112, 115–16, 121, 125
  education in, 34, 36, 40
  ethical dilemmas and decision-making in, 37–40
  ethical perspectives, 30–40, 43, 83
  as evidence-based, 102
  Kantian ethics in, 85
  spirituality in, 31–36
  theoretical perspectives, 105
  Ubuntu philosophy in, 88, 89, 90, 141
Solomon, Robert, 32
Speth, Gus, 33
Spirituality, 31–36
Statute of Charitable Uses 1601. *See* Statute of Elizabeth of 1601
Statute of Elizabeth of 1601, 13, 14, 16, 19, 23–24, 24, 47, 48–49, 52
Stetzar, Ed, 3
Sticker, Martin, 87
Sustainability, 69–70, 113–14
Sustainable Development Goals (SDGs), 75–76, 78
Swanepoel, Hennie, 5, 45
Swarbrick, David, 23
Swedberg, Richard, 60

Tacey, David, 32
Teleological ethics, 38–39, 83. *See also* Utilitarian ethics
Tenney, Merrill, 11
Theology. *See* Catholic theology; Pastoral theology; Protestant theology
Thompson, Mel, 2–3, 42, 44
Training and Resources in Research Ethics Evaluation (TRREE), 63
Transparency, 48–50, 52, 71, 72, 73, 80, 81, 99, 106–10
Transport and communication, 77, 107
Triangulation, as research methodology, 57–58, 132

# Index

Tribalism, 67, 69, 94, 100
TRREE. *See* Training and Resources in Research Ethics Evaluation (TRREE)
True needs (of the people), 75–78, 84, 87, 97–98, 107–10, 116–17, 119, 127–30, 133
Tutu, Desmond, 89, 92

Ubuntu philosophy, 12–13, 88–94, 97–98, 99–100
UNESCO World Heritage List, 17
UNICEF, 16
United Nations Conference on Trade and Development, 77
Unrepresented Nations and Peoples Organisation (UNPO), 44
Untruthfulness, 98–99
Utilitarian ethics, 30, 39, 83, 88, 105

Vilanti, Daniela, 33
Villegas, Diana, 32
Villiers, Pieter de, 32
Vodo, Teuta, 16
Vorster, Jakobus, 41

Walker, Lorraine, 123
Walla, Alice, 84

Warren, Rick, 56, 116
Wempe, Johan, 87
Wildlife conservation charities, 18
Wyk, Jan van, 41

Yahaya, Abubakar, 77–78
Yardley, Sue, 114

Zambia
  as a case study, ix–xi, xv–xvi, 1–4, 62, 137–139
  charity, definition of, 14, 15, 19
  as a Christian nation, 36, 79
  health charities in, 17
  Keeping Girls in School, 16
  NGOs, lack of policy, 2, 72–73, 117–118, 131, 137
  philanthropic strategies, failures, 94–101
  transparency and accountability, 48–49
  tribalism and, 69
  Ubuntu philosophy, 89–90
  wildlife conservation charities, 18
Zimbabwe, 4
  *See also* Mongu district

www.ingramcontent.com/pod-product-compliance
Lightning Source LLC
Chambersburg PA
CBHW071459150426
43191CB00008B/1392